KU-215-409

PUFFIN BOOKS

THE 13 CLOCKS
AND
THE WONDERFUL O

The 13 Clocks is a mixture of fairy tale, parable, and poetry. It
has everything in it to please everybody. There is a princess in
distress, a prince in disguise, a wicked uncle, and a last-minute
race between good and evil which is as exciting as any thriller.
James Thurber wrote it, when he was supposed to be writing
something quite different, because he couldn't help himself,
which must be why it bubbles with gaiety and wit, and why
everybody who has read it immediately wants to read it all over
again.

The Wonderful O, the second story in this book, is about two
abominable villains, a man with a map and a man with a ship,
who sail to the island of Ooroo in search of treasure and, when
they can't find it, revenge themselves on the gentle inhabitants
by banning everything with an O in it. First they take O's out
of all the words and then they start forbidding such things as
dogs, cottages, coconuts, and dolls. They are just getting round
to forbidding mothers when the islanders decide there are four
things with an O in them that must not be lost. Three of them
are 'hope' and 'love' and 'valour'. The fourth and most import-
ant is really the whole point of *The Wonderful O*, which is a
wonderful book.

We are proud to have these stories in our Puffin series; we are
pleased Ronald Searle has illustrated them for us; and we are
sure all readers of all ages will enjoy them.

James Thurber was born at Colombus, Ohio in 1894. For many
years he was a newspaperman, and much of his adult material
first appeared in the *New Yorker*. He was regarded as the greatest
American humorist, and did his own very individual drawings
to illustrate his work. He died in 1961, in New York.

JAMES THURBER

THE 13 CLOCKS
AND
THE WONDERFUL O

ILLUSTRATED BY
RONALD SEARLE

PUFFIN BOOKS
IN ASSOCIATION WITH
HAMISH HAMILTON

Puffin Books, Penguin Books Ltd, Harmondsworth, Middlesex, England
Viking Penguin Inc., 40 West 23rd Street, New York, New York 10010, U.S.A.
Penguin Books Australia Ltd, Ringwood, Victoria, Australia
Penguin Books Canada Limited, 2801 John Street, Markham, Ontario, Canada L3R 1B4
Penguin Books (N.Z.) Ltd, 182–190 Wairau Road, Auckland 10, New Zealand

—

The 13 Clocks first published by
Hamish Hamilton 1951
Copyright © James Thurber, 1951
The Wonderful O first published by
Hamish Hamilton 1958
Copyright © James Thurber, 1958
Published in Puffin Books 1962
Reprinted 1965, 1967, 1968, 1970, 1972, 1974, 1975, 1978, 1981,
1983, 1985, 1986

—

Made and printed in Great Britain
by Richard Clay (The Chaucer Press) Ltd,
Bungay, Suffolk
Set in Monotype Fournier

The
13
clocks

To Jap and Helen Gude
who have broken more than one
spell cast upon the author
by a witch or wizard,
this book is warmly
dedicated

ONCE upon a time, in a gloomy castle on a lonely hill, where there were thirteen clocks that wouldn't go, there lived a cold, aggressive Duke, and his niece, the Princess Saralinda. She was warm in every wind and weather, but he was always cold. His hands were as cold as his smile and almost as cold as his heart. He wore gloves when he was asleep, and he wore gloves when he was awake, which made it difficult for him to pick up pins or coins or the kernels of nuts, or to tear the wings from nightingales. He was six feet four, and forty-six, and even colder than he thought he was. One eye wore a velvet patch; the other glittered through a monocle, which made half his body seem closer to you than the other half. He had lost one eye when he was twelve, for he was fond of peering into nests and lairs in search of birds and animals to maul. One afternoon, a mother shrike had mauled him first. His nights were spent in evil dreams, and his days were given to wicked schemes.

Wickedly scheming, he would limp and cackle through the cold corridors of the castle, planning new impossible feats for the suitors of Saralinda to perform. He did not wish to give her hand in marriage, since her hand was the only warm hand in the castle. Even the hands of his watch and the hands of all the thirteen clocks were frozen. They had all frozen at the same time, on a snowy night, seven years before, and after that it was always ten minutes to five in the castle. Travellers and mariners would look up at the gloomy castle on the lonely hill and say, 'Time lies frozen there. It's always Then. It's never Now.'

The cold Duke was afraid of Now, for Now has warmth and urgency, and Then is dead and buried. Now might bring a certain knight of gay and shining courage – 'But, no!' the cold Duke muttered. 'The Prince will break himself against a new and awful labour: a place too high to reach, a thing too far to find, a burden too heavy to lift.' The Duke was afraid of Now, but he tampered with the clocks to see if they would go, out of a strange perversity, praying that they wouldn't. Tinkers and tinkerers and a few wizards who happened by tried to start the clocks with tools or magic words, or by shaking them and cursing, but nothing whirred or ticked. The clocks were dead, and in the end, brooding on it, the Duke decided he had murdered time, slain it with his sword, and wiped his bloody blade upon its beard and left it lying there, bleeding hours and minutes, its springs uncoiled and sprawling, its pendulum disintegrating.

The Duke limped because his legs were of different lengths. The right one had outgrown the left because, when he was young, he had spent his mornings place-kicking pups and punting kittens. He would say to a suitor, 'What is the difference in the length of my legs?' and if the youth replied, 'Why, one is shorter than the other,' the Duke would run him through with the sword he carried in his sword-cane and feed him to the geese. The suitor was supposed to say, 'Why, one is longer than the other.' Many a prince had been run through for naming the wrong difference. Others had been slain for offences equally trivial: trampling the Duke's camellias, failing to praise his wines, staring too long at his gloves, gazing too long at his niece. Those who survived his scorn and sword were given incredible labours to perform in order to win his niece's hand, the only warm hand in the castle, where time had frozen to death at ten minutes to five one snowy night. They were told to cut a slice of moon, or change the ocean into wine. They were set to finding things that never were, and building things that could not be. They came and tried and failed and disappeared and never came again. And some, as I have said, were slain, for using names that start with X, or dropping spoons, or wearing rings, or speaking disrespectfully of sin.

The castle and the Duke grew colder, and Saralinda, as a princess will, even in a place where time lies frozen, became a little older, but only a little older. She was nearly twenty-one the day a prince, disguised as a minstrel, came singing to the town that lay below the castle. He called himself Xingu, which was not his name, and dangerous, since the name began with X – and still does. He was, quite properly, a thing of shreds and patches, a ragged minstrel, singing for pennies and the love of singing. Xingu, as he so rashly called himself, was the youngest son of a powerful king, but he had grown weary of rich attire and banquets and tournaments and the available princesses of his own realm, and yearned to find in a far land the maiden of his dreams, singing as he went, learning the life of the lowly, and possibly slaying a dragon here and there.

At the sign of the Silver Swan, in the town below the castle, where taverners, travellers, taletellers, tosspots, troublemakers, and other townspeople were gathered, he heard of Saralinda, loveliest princess on all the thousand islands of the ocean seas. 'If you can turn the rain to silver, she is yours,' a taverner leered.

'If you can slay the thorny Boar of Borythorn, she is yours,' grinned a traveller. 'But there is no thorny Boar of Borythorn, which makes it hard.'

'What makes it even harder is her uncle's scorn and sword,' sneered a tale-teller. 'He will slit you from your guggle to your zatch.'

'The Duke is seven feet, nine inches tall, and only twenty-eight years old, or in his prime,' a tosspot gurgled. 'His hand is cold enough to stop a clock, and strong enough to choke a bull, and swift enough to catch the wind. He breaks up minstrels in his soup, like crackers.'

'Our minstrel here will warm the old man's heart with song, dazzle him with jewels and gold,' a troublemaker simpered. 'He'll trample on the Duke's camellias, spill his wine, and blunt his sword, and say his name begins with X, and in the end the Duke will say, "Take Saralinda, with my blessing, O lordly Prince of Rags and Tags, O rider of the sun!"'

The troublemaker weighed eighteen stone, but the minstrel picked him up and tossed him in the air and caught him and set him down again. Then he paid his due and left the Swan.

'I've seen that youth before,' the traveller mused, staring after Xingu, 'but he was neither ragamuffin then, nor minstrel. Now let me see, where was it?'

'In his soup,' the tosspot said, 'like crackers.'

2

OUTSIDE the tavern the night was lighted
by a rocking yellow moon that held a
white star in its horn. In the gloomy
castle on the hill a lantern gleamed and darkened,
came and went, as if the gaunt Duke stalked from
room to room, stabbing bats and spiders, killing

mice. 'Dazzle the Duke with jewels,' the minstrel said aloud. 'There's something in it somewhere, but what it is and where, I cannot think.' He wondered if the Duke would order him to cause a fall of purple snow, or make a table out of sawdust, or merely slit him from his guggle to his zatch, and say to Saralinda, 'There he lies, your latest fool, a nameless minstrel. I'll have my varlets feed him to the geese.' The minstrel shuddered in the moonlight, wondered where his zatch and guggle were. He wondered how and why and when he could invade the castle. A duke was never known to ask a ragged minstrel to his table, or set a task for him to do, or let him meet a princess. 'I'll think of some way,' thought the Prince. 'I'll think of something.'

The hour was late, and revellers began to reel and stagger home from inns and taverns, none in rags, and none in tags, and some in velvet gowns. One-third of the dogs in town began to bark. The minstrel took his lute from his shoulder and improvised a song. He had thought of something.

> 'Hark, hark, the dogs do bark,
>   But only one in three.
>   They bark at those in velvet gowns,
>   They never bark at me.'

A tale-teller, tottering home to bed, laughed at the song, and troublemakers and tosspots began to gather and listen.

> 'The Duke is fond of velvet gowns,
>   He'll ask you all to tea.
> But I'm in rags, and I'm in tags,
>   He'll never send for me.'

The townspeople crowded around the minstrel, laughing and cheering. 'He's a bold one, Rags is, makin' songs about the Duke!' giggled a strut-furrow who had joined the crowd. The minstrel went on singing.

> 'Hark, hark, the dogs do bark,
>   The Duke is fond of kittens.
> He likes to take their insides out,
>   And use their fur for mittens.'

The crowd fell silent in awe and wonder, for the townspeople knew the Duke had slain eleven men for merely staring at his hands, hands that were gloved in velvet gloves, bright with rubies and with diamonds. Fearing to be seen in the doomed and desperate company of the mad minstrel, the revellers slunk off to their homes to tell their wives. Only the traveller, who thought he had seen the singer some otherwhere and time, lingered to warn him of his peril. 'I've seen you shining in the lists,' he said, 'or toppling knights in battle, or breaking men in two like crackers. You must be Tristram's son, or Lancelot's, or are you Tyne or Tora?'

'A wandering minstrel, I,' the minstrel said, 'a thing of shreds and zatches.' He bit his tongue in consternation at the slip it made.

'Even if you were the mighty Zorn of Zorna,' said the man, 'you could not escape the fury of the Duke. He'll slit you from your guggle to your zatch, from here to here.' He touched the minstrel's stomach and his throat.

'I now know what to guard,' the minstrel sighed.

A black figure in velvet mask and hood and cloak disappeared behind a tree. 'The cold Duke's spy-in-chief,' the traveller said, 'a man named Whisper. Tomorrow he will die.' The minstrel waited. 'He'll die because, to name your sins, he'll have to mention mittens. I leave at once for other lands, since I have mentioned mittens.' He sighed. 'You'll never live to wed his niece. You'll only die to feed his geese. Good-bye, good night, and sorry.'

The traveller vanished, like a fly in the mouth of a frog, and the minstrel was left alone in the dark, deserted street. Somewhere a clock dropped a stony chime into the night. The minstrel began to sing again. A soft finger touched his shoulder and he turned to see a little man smiling in the moonlight. He wore an indescribable hat, his eyes were wide and astonished, as if everything were happening for the first time, and he had a dark, describable beard. 'If you have nothing better than your songs,' he said, 'you are somewhat less than much, and only a little more than anything.'

'I manage in my fashion,' the minstrel said, and he strummed his lute and sang.

> 'Hark, hark, the dogs do bark,
> The cravens are going to bed.
> Some will rise and greet the sun,
> But Whisper will be dead.'

The old man lost his smile.

'Who are you?' the minstrel asked.

'I am the Golux,' said the Golux, proudly, 'the only Golux in the world, and not a mere Device.'

'You resemble one,' the minstrel said, 'as Saralinda resembles the rose.'

'I resemble only half the things I say I don't,'

the Golux said. 'The other half resemble me.' He sighed. 'I must always be on hand when people are in peril.'

'My peril is my own,' the minstrel said.

'Half of it is yours and half is Saralinda's.'

'I hadn't thought of that,' the minstrel said. 'I place my faith in you, and where you lead, I follow.'

'Not so fast,' the Golux said. 'Half the places I have been to, never were. I make things up. Half the things I say are there cannot be found. When I was young I told a tale of buried gold, and men from leagues around dug in the woods. I dug myself.'

'But why?'

'I thought the tale of treasure might be true.'

'You said you made it up.'

'I know I did, but then I didn't know I had. I forget things, too.' The minstrel felt a vague uncertainty. 'I make mistakes, but I am on the side of Good,' the Golux said, 'by accident and happenchance. I had high hopes of being Evil when I was two, but in my youth I came upon a firefly burning in a spider's web. I saved the victim's life.'

Ronald Searle

'The firefly's?' said the minstrel.

'The spider's. The blinking arsonist had set the web on fire.' The minstrel's uncertainty increased, but as he thought to slip away, a deep bell sounded in the castle and many lights appeared, and voices shouted orders and commands. A stream of lanterns started flowing down the darkness. 'The Duke has heard your songs,' the Golux said. 'The fat is in the fire, the die is cast, the jig is up, the goose is cooked, and the cat is out of the bag.'

'My hour has struck,' the minstrel said. They heard a faint and distant rasping sound, as if a blade of steel were being sharpened on a stone.

'The Duke prepares to feed you to his geese,' the Golux said. 'We must invent a tale to stay his hand.'

'What manner of tale?' the minstrel asked.

'A tale', the Golux said, 'to make the Duke believe that slaying you would light a light in someone else's heart. He hates a light in people's hearts. So you must say a certain prince and princess can't be wed until the evening of the second day after the Duke has fed you to his geese.'

'I wish that you would not keep saying that,' the minstrel said.

'The tale sounds true,' the Golux said, 'and very like a witch's spell. The Duke has awe of witches' spells. I'm certain he will stay his hand, I think.'

The sound of tramping feet came near and nearer. The iron guards of the Duke closed in, their lanterns gleaming and their spears and armour. 'Halt!' There was a clang and clanking.

'Do not arrest my friend,' the youth implored.

'What friend?' the captain growled.

The minstrel looked around him and about, but there was no one there. A guard guffawed and said, 'Maybe he's seen the Golux.'

'There isn't any Golux. I have been to school, and know,' the captain said. The minstrel's uncertainty increased again. 'Fall in!' the captain bawled. 'Dress up that line.'

'You heard him. Dress it up,' the sergeant said. They marched the minstrel to the dungeon in the castle. A stream of lantern light flowed slowly up the hill.

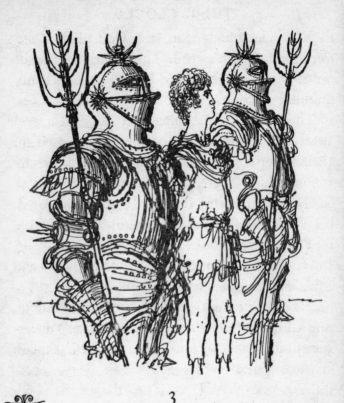

3

T was morning. The cold Duke gazed out
a window of the castle, as if he were watching flowers in bloom or flying birds. He
was watching his varlets feeding Whisper to the
geese. He turned away and took three limps and
stared at the minstrel, standing in the great hall of

the castle, both hands bound behind him. 'What manner of prince is this you speak of, and what manner of maiden does he love, to use a word that makes no sense and has no point?' His voice sounded like iron dropped on velvet.

'A noble prince, a noble lady,' the minstrel said. 'When they are wed a million people will be glad.'

The Duke took his sword out of his sword-cane and stared at it. He limped across and faced his captive, and touched his guggle softly with the point, and touched his zatch, and sighed and frowned, and put the sword away. 'We shall think of some amusing task for you to do,' he said. 'I do not like your tricks and guile. I think there is no prince or maiden who would wed if I should slay you, but I am neither sure nor certain.' He grinned and said again, 'We'll think of some amusing task for you to do.'

'But I am not a prince,' the minstrel said, 'and only princes may aspire to Saralinda's hand.'

The cold Duke kept on grinning. 'Why, then we'll make a prince of you,' he said. 'The prince of Rags and Jingles.' He clapped his gloves together and two varlets appeared without a word or sound. 'Take him to his dungeon,' said the

Duke. 'Feed him water without bread, and bread without water.'

The varlets were taking the minstrel out of the great hall when down the marble stairs the Princess Saralinda floated like a cloud. The Duke's eye gleamed like crystal. The minstrel gazed in wonder. The Princess Saralinda was tall, with freesias in her dark hair, and she wore serenity brightly like the rainbow. It was not easy to tell her mouth from the rose, or her brow from the white lilac. Her voice was faraway music, and her eyes were candles burning on a tranquil night. She moved across the room like wind in violets, and her laughter sparkled on the air, which, from her presence, gained a faint and undreamed fragrance. The Prince was frozen by her beauty, but not cold, and the Duke, who was cold but not frozen, held up the palms of his gloves, as if she were a fire at which to warm his hands. The minstrel saw the blood come warmly to the lame man's cheeks. 'This thing of rags and tags and tatters will play our little game,' he told his niece, his voice like iron on velvet.

'I wish him well,' the Princess said.

The minstrel broke his bonds and took her

hand in his, but it was slashed away by the swift cane of the Duke. 'Take him to his dungeon now,' he said. He stared coldly at the minstrel through his monocle. 'You'll find the most amusing bats and spiders there.'

'I wish him well,' the Princess said again, and the varlets took the minstrel to his dungeon.

When the great iron door of the dungeon clanked behind the minstrel, he found himself alone in blackness. A spider, swinging on a strand of web, swung back and forth. The zickering of bats was echoed by the walls. The minstrel took a step, avoiding snakes, and something squirmed. 'Take care,' the Golux said, 'you're on my foot.'

'Why are you here?' the minstrel cried.

'I forgot something. I forgot about the task the Duke will set you.'

The minstrel thought of swimming lakes too wide to swim, of turning liquids into stone, or finding boneless creatures made of bone. 'How came you here?' he asked. 'And can you leave?'

'I never know,' the Golux said. 'My mother was a witch, but rather mediocre in her way. When she tried to turn a thing to gold, it turned to clay; and when she changed her rivals into fish, all she ever got was mermaids.' The minstrel's heart was insecure. 'My father was a wizard,' said his friend, 'who often cast his spells upon himself, when he was in his cups. Strike a light or light a lantern! Something I have hold of has no head.'

The minstrel shuddered. 'The task,' he said. 'You came to tell me.'

'I did? Oh, yes. My father lacked the power of concentration, and that is bad for monks and priests, and worse for wizards. Listen. Tell the Duke that you will hunt the Boar, or travel thrice around the moon, or turn November into June. Implore him not to send you out to find a thousand jewels.'

'And then?'

'And then he'll send you out to find a thousand jewels.'

'But I am poor!' the minstrel cried.

'Come, come,' the Golux said. 'You're Zorn of Zorna. I had it from a traveller I met. It came to him as he was leaving town. Your father's casks and coffers shine with rubies and with sapphires.'

'My father lives in Zorna,' said the Prince, 'and it would take me nine and ninety days: three and

thirty days to go, and three and thirty days to come back here.'

'That's six and sixty.'

'It always takes my father three and thirty days to make decisions,' said the Prince. 'In spells and labours a certain time is always set, and I might be at sea when mine expires.'

'That's another problem for another day,' the Golux said. 'Time is for dragonflies and angels. The former live too little and the latter live too long.'

Zorn of Zorna thought awhile and said, 'The task seems strange and simple.'

'There are no jewels', the Golux said, 'within the reach and ranges of this island, except the gems here in this castle. The Duke knows not that you are Zorn of Zorna. He thinks you are a minstrel without a penny or a moonstone. He's fond of jewels. You've seen them on his gloves.'

The Prince stepped on a turtle. 'The Duke has spies,' he said, 'who may know who I am.'

The Golux sighed. 'I may be wrong,' he said, 'but we must risk and try it.'

The Prince sighed in his turn. 'I wish you could be surer.'

'I wish I could,' the Golux said. 'My mother was born, I regret to say, only partly in a caul. I've saved a score of princes in my time. I cannot save them all.' Something that would have been purple, if there had been light to see it by, scuttled across the floor. 'The Duke might give me only thirty days, or forty-two, to find a thousand jewels,' said Zorn of Zorna. 'Why should he give me ninety-nine?'

'The way I figure it', the Golux said, 'is this. The longer the labour lasts, the longer lasts his gloating. He loves to gloat, you know.'

The Prince sat down beside a toad. 'My father may have lost his jewels,' he said, 'or given them away.'

'I thought of that,' the Golux said. 'But I have other plans than one. Right now we have to sleep.'

They found a corner without creatures and slept until the town clock struck the midnight hour.

Chains clanked and rattled, and the great iron door began to move. 'The Duke has sent for you again,' the Golux said. 'Be careful what you say and what you do.'

The great iron door began to open slowly. 'When shall I see you next?' Zorn whispered. There was no answer. The Prince groped around in the dark and felt a thing very like a cat, and touched the thing without a head, but he could not find the Golux.

The great iron door was open wide now and the dungeon filled with lantern light.

'The Duke commands your presence,' growled a guard. 'What was *that*?'

'What was what?'

'I know not,' said the guard. 'I thought I heard the sound of someone laughing.'

'Is the Duke afraid of laughter?' asked the Prince.

'The Duke is not afraid of anything. Not even', said the guard, 'the Todal.'

'The Todal?'

'The Todal.'

'What's the Todal?'

A lock of the guard's hair turned white and his teeth began to chatter. 'The Todal looks like a blob of glup,' he said. 'It makes a sound like rabbits screaming, and smells of old, unopened rooms. It's waiting for the Duke to fail in some endeavour, such as setting you a task that you can do.'

'And if he sets me one, and I succeed?' the Prince inquired.

'The Blob will glup him,' said the guard. 'It's an agent of the devil, sent to punish evildoers for having done less evil than they should. I talk too much. Come on. The Duke is waiting.'

4

THE Duke sat at one end of a black oak table in the black oak room, lighted by flaming torches that threw red gleams on shields and lances. The Duke's gloves sparkled when he moved his hands. He stared moodily through his monocle at young Prince Zorn. The

Duke sneered, which made him even colder. 'So you would hunt the Boar,' he said, 'or travel thrice around the moon, or turn November into June.' He laughed, and a torch went out. 'Saralinda in November turns November into June. A cow can travel thrice around the moon, or even more. And *anyone* can merely *hunt* the Boar. I have another plan for you. I thought it up myself last night, while I was killing mice. I'll send you out to find a thousand jewels and bring them back.'

The Prince turned pale, or tried to. 'A wandering minstrel, I,' he said, 'a thing of –'

'Rubies and sapphires.' The Duke's chuckle sounded like ice cackling in a cauldron. 'For you are Zorn of Zorna,' he whispered, softly. 'Your father's casks and vaults and coffers shine with jewels. In six and sixty days you could sail to Zorna and return.'

'It always takes my father three and thirty days to make decisions,' cried the Prince.

The Duke grinned. 'That is what I wanted to know, my naïve Prince,' he said. 'Then you would have me give you nine and ninety days?'

'That would be fair,' the Prince replied. 'But how do you know that I am Zorn?'

'I have a spy named Hark,' the Duke explained, 'who found your princely raiment in your quarters in the town and brought it here, with certain signs and seals and signatures, revealing who you are. Go put the raiment on.' He pointed at a flight of iron stairs. 'You'll find it in a chamber on whose door a star is turning black. Don it and return. I'll think of beetles while you're gone, and things like that.' The Duke limped to his chair and sat down again, and the Prince started up the iron stairs, wondering where the Golux was. He stopped and turned and said, 'You will not give me nine and ninety days. How many, then?' The Duke sneered. 'I'll think of a lovely number,' he said. 'Go on.'

When Zorn came back he wore his royal attire, but the Duke's spies had sealed his sword, so that he could not draw it. The Duke sat staring at a man who wore a velvet mask and cloak and hood. 'This is Hark,' he said, 'and this is Listen.' He gestured with his cane at nothing.

'There's no one there,' said Zorn.

'Listen is invisible,' the Duke explained. 'Listen can be heard, but never seen. They are here to learn the mark and measure of your task. I give you nine and ninety hours, not nine and ninety days, to find a thousand jewels and bring them here. When you return, the clocks must all be striking five.'

'The clocks here in the castle?' asked the Prince. 'The thirteen clocks?'

'The clocks here in the castle,' said the Duke, 'the thirteen clocks.'

The Prince looked at the two clocks on the walls. Their hands pointed to ten minutes to five. 'The hands are frozen,' said the Prince. 'The clocks are dead.'

'Precisely,' said the Duke, 'and what is more, which makes your task a charming one, there are no jewels that could be found within the space of nine and ninety hours, except those in my vaults, and these.' He held his gloves up and they sparkled.

'A pretty task,' said Hark.

'Ingenious,' said the voice of Listen.

'I thought you'd like it,' said the Duke. 'Unseal his sword.' Invisible hands unsealed the Prince's sword.

'And if I should succeed?' asked Zorn.

The Duke waved a gloved hand at the iron

stairs, and Zorn saw Saralinda standing there. 'I wish him well,' she said, and her uncle laughed and looked at Zorn. 'I hired a witch', he said, 'to cast a tiny spell upon her. When she is in my presence, all that she can say is this: "I wish him well." You like it?'

'A clever spell,' said Hark.

'An awful spell,' the voice of Listen said.

The Prince and Princess spoke a silent language with their eyes, until the Duke cried, 'Go!' and Saralinda vanished up the stairs.

'And if I fail?' asked Zorn.

The Duke removed his sword from his sword-cane and ran his glove along the blade. 'I'll slit you from your guggle to your zatch, and feed you to the Todal.'

'I've heard of it,' said Zorn.

The Duke smiled. 'You've only heard of half of it,' he said. 'The other half is worse. It's made of lip. It feels as if it had been dead at least a dozen days, but it moves about like monkeys and like shadows.' The Prince took out his sword and put it back. 'The Todal can't be killed,' the Duke said, softly.

'It gleeps,' said Hark.

'What's gleeping?' asked the Prince.

The Duke and Hark and Listen laughed. 'Time is wasting, Prince,' the Duke reminded him. 'Already you have only eight and ninety hours. I wish you every strangest kind of luck.' A wide oak door suddenly opened at the end of the room, and the Prince saw lightning and midnight and falling rain. 'One last word and warning,' said the Duke. 'I would not trust the Golux overfar. He cannot tell what can be from what can't. He seldom knows what should be from what is.'

The Prince glanced at Hark and at the Duke, and at a spot where he thought Listen stood. 'When all the clocks are striking five,' he said, and left the room. The laughter of the Duke and Hark and Listen followed him out the door and down the stairs and into the darkness. When he had gone a few steps from the castle, he looked up at a lighted window and thought he saw the Princess Saralinda standing there. A rose fell at his feet, and as he picked it up, the laughter of the Duke and Hark and Listen increased inside the black oak room and died away.

5

THE Prince had gone but a short way from the castle when he felt a gentle finger touch his elbow. 'It is the Golux,' said the Golux, proudly. 'The only Golux in the world.'

The Prince was in no mood for the old man's

gaiety and cheer. The Golux did not seem wonderful to him now, and even his indescribable hat was suddenly describable. 'The Duke thinks you are not so wise as he thinks you think you are,' he said.

The Golux smiled. 'I think he is not so wise as he thinks I think he is,' he said. 'I was there. I know the terms. I had thought that only dragonflies and angels think of time, never having been an angel or a dragonfly.'

'How were you there?' the Prince said in surprise.

'I am Listen,' the Golux said, 'or at any rate, he thinks I am. Never trust a spy you cannot see. The Duke is lamer than I am old, and I am shorter than he is cold, but it comes to you with some surprise that I am wiser than he is wise.'

The Prince's courage began to return. 'I think you are the most remarkable man in the world,' he said.

'Who thought not so a moment since, knows not the apple from the quince,' the Golux said. He scowled. 'We now have only eight and ninety *hours* to find a thousand gems,' he said.

'You said that you had other plans than one,' the Prince reminded him.

'What plans?' the Golux asked.

'You didn't say,' said Zorn.

The Golux closed his eyes and clasped his hands. 'There was a treasure ship that sank, not more than forty hours from here,' he said. 'But, come to think of it, the Duke ransacked the ship and stole the jewels.'

'So much', sighed Zorn, 'for that.'

The Golux thought again. 'If there were hail,' he said, 'and we could stain the hail with blood, it might turn into rubies.'

'There is no hail,' said Zorn.

The Golux sighed. 'So much', he said, 'for that.'

'The task is hard', said Zorn, 'and can't be done.'

'I can do a score of things that can't be done,' the Golux said. 'I can find a thing I cannot see and see a thing I cannot find. The first is time, the second is a spot before my eyes. I can feel a thing I cannot touch and touch a thing I cannot feel. The first is sad and sorry, the second is your heart. What would you do without me? Say "nothing".'

'Nothing,' said the Prince.

'Good. Then you're helpless and I'll help you. I said I had another plan than one, and I have just remembered what it is. There is a woman on this isle, who'd have some eight and eighty years, and she is gifted with the strangest gift of all. For when she weeps, what do you think she weeps?'

'Tears,' said Zorn.

'Jewels,' said the Golux.

The Prince stared at him. 'But that is too remarkable to be,' he said.

'I don't see why,' the Golux said. 'Even the lowly oyster makes his pearls without the use of eyes or hands or any tools, and pearls are jewels. The oyster is a blob of glup, but a woman is a woman.'

The Prince thought of the Todal and felt a small cold feeling in his guggle. 'Where does this wondrous woman dwell?' he asked.

The old man groaned. 'Over mountain, over stream, by the way of storm and thunder, in a hut so high or deep – I never can remember which – the naked eye can't see it.' He stood up. 'We must be on our way,' he said. 'It will take us ninety hours, or more or less, to go and come. It's this way, or it's that way. Make up my mind.'

'How can I?' asked the Prince. 'You have a rose,' the Golux said. 'Hold it in your hand.' The Prince took out the rose and held it in his hand, and its stem slowly turned and stopped. 'It's this way,' cried the Golux, and they started off in the direction the stem of the rose had pointed out. 'I will tell you the tale of Hagga,' said the Golux.

When Hagga was eleven (he began) and picking cherries in the woods one day, and asphodel, she came upon the good King Gwain of Yarrow with his foot caught in a wolf trap. 'Weep for me, maiden,' said the King, 'for I am ludicrous and laughable, with my foot caught in this trap. I am no longer ert, for I have lost my ertia. By twiddling my fingers or clapping my hands, I have often changed the fate of men, but now I cannot get my foot loose from this thing.'

'I have no time for tears,' the maiden said. She knew the secret of the trap, and was about to free the fettered foot, when a farmer from a near-by farm began to laugh. The King beshrewed him and his wife, and turned them into grasshoppers, creatures that look as if their feet are caught in traps, even when they aren't.

'Lo, the maid has freed my foot,' the King exulted, seeing that she had, 'but it is numb, and feels like someone else's foot, not mine.' The maiden took off his shoe and rubbed his foot, until it felt like his and he could put it down. And for her kindness the grateful King gave her the power to weep jewels when she wept, instead of tears. When the people learned of the strange gift the King had given Hagga, they came from leagues around, by night and day, in warm and winter weather, to make her sad and sorry. Nothing tragic happened but she heard of it and wept. People came with heavy hearts and left with pearls and rubies. Paths were paved with pearls, and rivers ran with rubies. Children played with sapphires in the streets, and dogs chewed opals. Every peacock had at least nine diamonds in its gizzard, and one, cut open on St Wistow's Day, had thirty-eight. The price of stones and pebbles rose, the price of gems declined, until, for making Hagga weep, you could be hanged and fined. In the end, the jewels were melted, in a frightful fire, by order of the King. 'I will make her weep myself, one day each year,' the King decreed, 'and thus and hence, the flow of gems will make some sense, and have some point and balance.' But alas, and but alack, the maid could weep no more at any tale of tragedy or tribulation. Damsels killed by dragons left her cold, and broken hearts, and children lost, and love denied. She never wept by day or night, in warm or winter weather. She grew to be sixteen, and twenty-six, and thirty-four, and forty-eight, and fifty-two, and now she waits, at eighty-eight, for me and you. 'I hope,' the Golux said, 'that this is true. I make things up, you know.'

The young Prince sighed and said, 'I know you do. If Hagga weeps no more, why should she weep for you?'

The Golux thought it over. 'I feel that she is frail and fragile. I trust that she is sad and sorry. I hope that she is neither dead nor dying. I'll think of something very sad to tell her. Very sad and lonely. Take out your rose, I think we're lost.'

They had become tangled in brambles by now, and the trees of the forest they had entered were tall and thick. Thorns began to tear the Prince's raiment. Lightning flashed and thunder rolled,

47

and all paths vanished. The Prince took out the rose and held it in his hand. The stem began to turn and twist, and pointed.

'Around this way,' the Golux said. 'It's lighter here.' He found a narrow path that led straight onward. As they walked along the path, the Golux leading, they met a Jackadandy, whose clothes were torn and tattered.

'I told my tales to Hagga,' said the man; 'but Hagga weeps no more. I told her tales of lovers lost in April. I told her tales of maidens dead in June. I told her tales of princes fed to geese. I even told her how I lost my youngest niece.'

'This is sad,' the Golux said, 'and getting sadder.'

'The way is long,' the torn man said, 'and getting longer. The road goes uphill all the way, and even farther. I wish you luck,' he said. 'You'll need it.' He disappeared in brambles.

The only light in the forest came from lightning, and when it flashed they watched the rose and followed where it pointed. This brought them, on the second day, into a valley. They saw a Jack-o'-lent approaching, his clothes all torn and tattered. 'I told my tales to Hagga,' said the man, 'but

Ronald Searle

Hagga weeps no more. I told her tales of lovers lost at sea and drowned in fountains. I told her tales of babies lost in woods and lost on mountains. She wept not,' said the Jack-o'-lent. 'The way is dark, and getting darker. The hut is high and even higher. I wish you luck. There is none.' He vanished in the briars.

The brambles and the thorns grew thick and thicker in a ticking thicket of bickering crickets. Farther along and stronger, bonged the gongs of a throng of frogs, green and vivid on their lily pads. From the sky came the crying of flies, and the pilgrims leaped over a bleating sheep creeping knee-deep in a sleepy stream, in which swift and slippery snakes slid and slithered silkily, whispering sinful secrets.

A comet whistled through the sky, and by its light they saw the hut of Hagga high on Hagga's hill. 'If she is dead, there may be strangers there,' the Golux said.

'How many hours do we have left?' the Prince demanded.

'If we can make her weep within the hour,' the Golux said, 'we'll barely make it.'

'I hope that she's alive and sad,' said Zorn.

'I feel that she has died,' the Golux sighed. 'I feel it in my stomach. You'd better carry me. I'm weary.'

Zorn of Zorna picked the Golux up and carried him.

6

IT was cold on Hagga's hill, and fresh with furrows where the dragging points of stars had ploughed the fields. A peasant in a purple smock stalked the smoking furrows, sowing seeds. There was a smell, the Golux thought, a little like Forever in the air, but mixed with something faint and less enduring, possibly the fragrance of a flower. 'There's no light in her window,' the Golux said, 'and it is dark and getting darker.'

'There's no smoke in her chimney,' said the Prince, 'and it is cold and getting colder.'

The Golux barely breathed and said, 'What worries me the most is that spider's web there on the door, that stretches from the hinges to the latch.'

The young Prince felt a hollow feeling in his zatch. 'Knock on her door,' the Golux said, his voice so high it quavered. He crossed his fingers and kept them crossed, and Zorn knocked on the door. No one answered. 'Knock again,' the Golux cried, and Prince Zorn knocked again.

Hagga was there. She came to the door and stared at them, a woman neither dead nor dying, and clearly only thirty-eight or thirty-nine. The Golux had missed her age by fifty years, as old men often do. 'Weep for us,' the Golux cried, 'or else this Prince will never wed his Princess.'

'I have no tears,' said Hagga. 'Once I wept when ships were overdue, or brooks ran dry, or tangerines were over-ripe, or sheep got something in their eye. I weep no more,' said Hagga.

Her eyes were dry as deserts and her mouth seemed made of stone. 'I have turned a thousand persons gemless from my door. Come in,' she said. 'I weep no more.'

The room was dark and held a table and a chair, and in one corner something like a chest, made of oak and bound with brass. The Golux smiled and then looked sad, and said, 'I have tales to make a hangman weep, and tales to bring a tear of sorrow to a monster's eye. I have tales that would disturb a dragon's sleep, and even make the Todal sigh.'

At the mention of the Todal, Hagga's hair turned grey. 'Once I wept when maids were married underneath the April moon. I weep no more when maids are buried, even in the month of June.'

'You have the emotions of a fish,' said the Golux, irritably. He sat on the floor and told her tales of the death of kings, and kindred things, and little children choked by rings.

'I have no tears,' said Hagga.

He told her tales of the frogs in the forum, and the toads in the rice that destroyed the poppy-cockalorum and the cockahoopatrice.

'I weep no more,' said Hagga.

'Look,' the Golux said, 'and listen! The Princess Saralinda will never wed this youth until the day he lays a thousand jewels upon a certain table.'

'I would weep for Saralinda,' Hagga sighed, 'if I were able.'

The Prince had wandered to the oaken chest. He seized its cover with his hand and threw it open. A radiance filled the room and lit the darkest corners. Inside the chest there were at least ten thousand jewels of the very sort and kind the Duke demanded. Diamonds flared and rubies glowed, and sapphires burned and emeralds seemed on fire. They looked at Hagga. 'These are the jewels of laughter,' Hagga said. 'I woke up fourteen days ago to find them on my bed. I had laughed until I wept at something in my sleep.' The Golux grabbed a gleaming handful of the gems, and then another, crowing with delight. 'Put them back,' said Hagga. 'For there's a thing that you must know, concerning jewels of laughter. They always turn again to tears a fortnight after. It has been a fortnight, to the day and minute, since I took the pretties to this chest and put them in it.'

Even as they watched, the light and colour

died. The diamonds dimmed, the emeralds went out, and the jewels of Hagga's laughter turned to tears, with a little sound like sighing. There was nothing in the chest but limpid liquid, leering up at them and winking. 'You must think,' the Golux cried. 'You must think of what you laughed at in your sleep.'

Hagga's eyes were blank. 'I do not know, for this was fourteen days ago.'

'Think!' the Golux said.

'Think!' said Zorn of Zorna.

Hagga frowned and said, 'I never can remember dreams.'

The Golux clasped his hands behind his back and thought it over. 'As I remember and recall,' he said, 'the jewels of sorrow last forever. Such was the gift and power the good Gwain gave you. What was he doing, by the way, so many leagues from Yarrow?'

'Hunting,' Hagga said. 'Wolves, as I recall it.'

The Golux scowled. 'I am a man of logic, in my way. What happened on that awful day, to make him value sorrow over and above the gift of laughter? Why have these jewels turned to tears a fortnight after?'

'There was a farmer from a near-by farm, who laughed,' said Hagga. ' "On second thought," the good King said, "I will amend and modify the gift I gave you. The jewels of sorrow will last beyond all measure, but may the jewels of laughter give you little pleasure." '

The Golux groaned. 'If there's one thing in the world I hate,' he said, 'it is amendments.' His eyes turned bright and brighter, and he clapped his hands. 'I will make her laugh until she weeps,' he said.

The Golux told her funny tales of things that were and had been, but Hagga's eyes were dry as quartz and her mouth seemed made of agate. 'I laugh at nothing that has been,' she said, 'or is.'

The Golux smiled. 'Then we will think of things that will be, and aren't now, and never were. I'll think of something,' and he thought, and thought of something.

> 'A dehoy who was terribly hobble,
> Cast only stones that were cobble
> And bats that were ding,
> From a shot that was sling,
> But never hit inks that were bobble.'

Hagga laughed until she wept, and seven moon-stones trickled down her cheek and clattered on the floor. 'She's weeping semi-precious stones!' the Golux wailed. He tried again:

> 'There was an old coddle so molly,
> He talked in a glot that was poly,
> His gaws were so gew
> That his laps became dew,
> And he ate only pops that were lolly.'

Hagga laughed until she wept, and seven brilliants trickled down her cheek and clattered on the floor. 'Rhinestones!' groaned the Golux. 'Now she's weeping costume jewellery!'

The young Prince tried his hand at telling tales of laughter, but for his pains he got a shower of tourmaline, a cat's-eye, and a flux of pearls. 'The Duke hates pearls,' the Golux moaned. 'He thinks they're made by fish.'

It grew darker in the room and they could scarcely see. The starlight and the moon were gone. They stood there, still as statues. The Golux cleared his throat. The Prince uncrossed his arms and crossed them. And then, without a rhyme or reason, out of time and out of season,

Hagga laughed and kept on laughing. No one had said a word, no one had told a tale. It might have been the hooting of an owl. It might have been the crawling of a snail. But Hagga laughed and kept on laughing, and precious jewels twinkled down her cheek and sparkled on the floor, until the hut was ankle-deep in diamonds and in rubies. The Golux counted out a thousand and put them in a velvet sack that he had brought along. 'I wish that she had laughed,' he sighed, 'at something I had said.'

Zorn of Zorna took her hand. 'God keep you warm in winter,' said the Prince, 'and cool in summer.'

'Farewell,' the Golux said, 'and thank you.'

Hagga laughed and kept on laughing, and sapphires burned upon the floor and lit the Golux towards the door.

'How many hours are left us now?' the young Prince cried. 'It's odd,' the Golux muttered to himself. 'I could have sworn that she had died. This is the only time my stomach ever lied.'

'How many hours are left us now?' the Prince implored.

Hagga sat upon the chest and kept on laughing.

'I should say', the Golux said, 'that we have only forty left, but it is downhill all the way.'

They went out into the moonless night and peered about them in the dark.

'I think it's this way,' the Golux said, and they went the way he thought it was.

'What about the clocks?' demanded Zorn.

The Golux exhaled a sorry breath. 'That's another problem for another hour,' he said.

Inside the hut, something red and larger than a ruby glowed among the jewels and Hagga picked it up. 'A rose,' she said. 'They must have dropped it.'

7

IN the black oak room the yellow torches flared and crackled on the walls, and their fire burned on the lances and the shields. The Duke's gloves glittered. 'How goes the night?' he gnarled.

'The moon is down,' said Hark. 'I have not heard the clocks.'

'You'll never hear them!' screamed the Duke. 'I slew time in this castle many a cold and snowy year ago.'

Hark stared at him emptily and seemed to be chewing something. 'Time froze here. Someone left the windows open.'

'Bah!' The Duke sat down at the far end of the table, stood up again, and limped about. 'It bled hours and minutes on the floor. I saw it with my eye.' Hark kept on chewing something. Outside the Gothic windows thunder growled. An owl flew by.

'There are no jewels,' roared the Duke. 'They'll have to bring me pebbles from the sea or mica from the meadows.' He gave his awful laugh. 'How goes the night?' he asked again.

'I have been counting off and on,' said Hark, 'and I should say they have some forty minutes left.'

'They'll never make it!' the cold Duke screamed. 'I hope they drowned, or broke their legs, or lost their way.' He came so close to Hark their noses almost touched. 'Where were they going?' he whispered harshly.

Hark stepped backwards seven steps. 'I met a

Jackadandy, some seven hours ago,' he said. 'They passed him on their way to Hagga's hill. Do you remember Hagga, and have you thought of her?'

The Duke's loud laughter rang the shields.

'Hagga weeps no more,' he said. 'Hagga has no tears. She did not even weep when she was told about the children locked up in my tower.'

'I hated that,' said Hark.

'I liked it,' said the Duke. 'No child can sleep in my camellias.' He began to limp again and stared out at the night. 'Where is Listen?' he demanded.

'He followed them,' said Hark, 'the Golux and the Prince.'

'I do not trust him,' growled the Duke. 'I like a spy that I can see. Let me have men about me that are visible.' He shouted 'Listen!' up the stairs, and 'Listen!' out of the windows, but no one answered. 'I'm cold,' he rasped.

'You always are.'

'I'm colder,' snarled the Duke, 'and never tell me what I always am!' He took his sword out and slashed at nothing and at silence. 'I miss Whisper.'

'You fed him to the geese,' said Hark. 'They seemed to like him.'

'Silence! What was that?'

'What did it sound like?'

'Like princes stealing up the stairs, like Saralinda leaving.' The Duke limped to the iron stairs and slashed again at silence and at nothing. 'What does he feel like? Have you felt him?'

'Listen? He's five feet high,' said Hark. 'He has a beard, and something on his head I can't describe.'

'The Golux!' shrieked the Duke. 'You felt the Golux! I hired him as a spy and didn't know it.'

A purple ball with gold stars on it came slowly bouncing down the iron stairs and winked and twinkled, like a naked child saluting priests. 'What insolence is this?' the Duke demanded. 'What is that thing?'

'A ball,' said Hark.

'I know that!' screamed the Duke. 'But why? What does its ghastly presence signify?'

'It looks to me', said Hark, 'very like a ball the Golux and those children used to play with.'

'They're on his side!' The Duke was apoplectic. 'Their ghosts are on his side.'

'He has a lot of friends,' said Hark.

'Silence!' roared the Duke. 'He knows not what is dead from what is dying, or where he's been from where he's going, or striking clocks from clocks that never strike.'

'What makes me think he does?' The spy stopped chewing. Something very much like nothing anyone had seen before came trotting down the stairs and crossed the room.

'What is that?' the Duke asked, palely.

'I don't know what it is,' said Hark, 'but it's the only one there ever was.'

The Duke's gloved hands shook and shimmered. 'I'll throw them up for grabs betwixt the Todal and the geese! I'll lock them in the dungeon with the thing without a head!' At the mention of the Todal, Hark's velvet mask turned grey. The Duke's eye twisted upwards in its socket. 'I'll slay them all!' he said. 'This sweetheart and her suitor, this cross-eyed clown! You hear me?'

'Yes,' said Hark, 'but there are rules and rites and rituals, older than the sound of bells and snow on mountains.'

'Go on,' the Duke said, softly, looking up the stairs.

'You must let them have their time and turn to make the castle clocks strike five.'

'The castle clocks were murdered,' said the Duke. 'I killed time here myself one snowy morning. You still can see the old brown stains, where seconds bled to death, here on my sleeve.' He laughed. 'What else?' he asked.

'You know as well as I,' said Hark. 'The Prince must have his turn and time to lay a thousand jewels there on the table.'

'And if he does?'

'He wins the hand of Princess Saralinda.'

'The only warm hand in the castle,' said the Duke. 'Who loses Saralinda loses fire. I mean the fire of the setting suns, and not the cold and cheerless flame of jewels. Her eyes are candles burning in a shrine. Her feet appear to me as doves. Her fingers bloom upon her breast like flowers.'

'This is scarcely the way,' said Hark, 'to speak of one's own niece.'

'She's not my niece! I stole her!' cried the Duke. 'I stole her from the castle of a king! I snatched her from the bosom of a sleeping queen. I still bear on my hands the marks of where she bit me.'

'The Queen?' asked Hark.

'The Princess,' roared the Duke.

'Who was the King?' asked Hark.

His master scowled. 'I never knew,' he said. 'My ship was beached upon an island in a storm. There was no moon or any star. No lights were in the castle.'

'How could you find the Princess then?' asked Hark.

'She had a radiance,' said the Duke. 'She shone there like a star upon her mother's breast. I knew I had to have that splendour in my castle. I mean to keep her here till she is twenty-one. The day she is, I'll wed her, and that day is tomorrow.'

'Why haven't you before?' asked Hark. 'This castle is your kingdom.'

The Duke smiled and showed his upper teeth. 'Because her nurse turned out to be a witch who cast a spell upon me.'

'What were its terms?' asked Hark.

'I cannot wed her till the day she's twenty-one, and that day is tomorrow.'

'You said that once before.'

'I must keep her in a chamber where she is safe from me. I've done that.'

'I like that part,' said Hark.

'I hate it,' snarled the Duke. 'I must give and grant the right to any prince to seek her hand in marriage. I've done that, too.' He sat down at the table.

'In spells of this sort,' Hark said, chewing, 'one always finds a chink or loophole, by means of which the right and perfect prince can win her hand in spite of any task you set him. How did the witch announce that part of it?'

'Like this. "She can be saved, and you destroyed, only by a prince whose name begins with X and doesn't." There is no prince whose name begins with X and doesn't.'

Hark's mask slipped off and he put it back again, but not before the Duke saw laughter in his eyes. 'This prince', said Hark, 'is Zorn of Zorna, but to your terror and distaste, he once posed as a minstrel. His name was Xingu then and wasn't. This is the prince whose name begins with X and doesn't.'

The Duke's sword had begun to shake. 'Nobody ever tells me anything,' he whispered to himself.

Another ball came bouncing down the stairs, a

black ball stamped with scarlet owls. The cold Duke watched it roll across the floor. 'What impudence is this?' he cried.

Hark walked to the stairs and listened, and turned and said, 'There's someone up there.'

'It's the children!' croaked the Duke.

'The children are dead,' said Hark, 'and the sound I heard was made by living feet.'

'How much time is left them?' cried the Duke.

'Half an hour, I think,' said Hark.

'I'll have their guggles on my sword for playing games with me!' The Duke started up the stairs and stopped. 'They're up there, all of them. Call out the guards,' he barked.

'The guards are guarding the clocks,' said Hark. 'You wanted it that way. There are eleven guards, and each one guards a clock. You and I are guarding *these*.' He pointed at the two clocks on the walls. 'You wanted it that way.'

'Call out the guards,' the Duke repeated, and his agent called the guards. They trooped into the room like engines. The Duke limped up the stairs, his drawn sword shining. 'Follow me!' he cried. 'Another game's afoot! I'll slay the Golux and the Prince, and marry Saralinda!' He led the way. The guards ramped up the stairs like engines. Hark smiled, and chewed again, and followed.

The black oak room was silent for a space of seven seconds. Then a secret door swung open in a wall. The Golux slipped into the room. The Princess followed. His hands were raw and red from climbing vines to Saralinda's chamber. 'How could you find the castle in the dark without my rose?' she asked. 'He would not let me burn a torch.'

'You lighted up your window like a star, and we could see the castle from afar,' the Golux said. 'Our time is marked in minutes. Start the clocks!'

'I cannot start the clocks,' the Princess said.

They heard the sound of fighting far above. 'He faces thirteen men,' she cried, 'and that is hard.'

'We face thirteen clocks,' the Golux said, 'and that is harder. Start the clocks!'

'How can I start the clocks?' the Princess wailed.

'Your hand is warmer than the snow is cold,' the Golux said. 'Touch the first clock with your hand.' The Princess touched it. Nothing happened. 'Again!' Saralinda held her hand against the clock and nothing happened. 'We are ruined,' said the Golux simply, and Saralinda's heart stood still.

She cried, 'Use magic!'

'I have no magic to depend on,' groaned the Golux. 'Try the other clock.'

The Princess tried the other clock and nothing happened. 'Use logic, then!' she cried. In the secret walls they heard the Iron Guard pounding after Zorn, and coming close.

'Now let me see,' the Golux said. 'If you can touch the clocks and never start them, then you can start the clocks and never touch them. That's logic, as I know and use it. Hold your hand this far away. Now that far. Closer! Now a little farther back. A little farther. There! I think you have it! Do not move!'

The clogged and rigid works of the clock began to whir. They heard a tick and then a ticking. The Princess Saralinda fled from room to room, like wind in clover, and held her hand the proper distance from the clocks. Something like a vulture spread its wings and left the castle. 'That was Then,' the Golux said.

'It's Now!' cried Saralinda.

A morning glory that had never opened, opened in the courtyard. A cock that never crowed, began to crow. The light of morning stained the windows, and in the walls the cold Duke moaned, 'I hear the sound of time. And yet I slew it, and wiped my bloody sword upon its beard.' He thought that Zorn of Zorna had escaped the guards. His sword kept whining in the blackness, and once he slashed his own left knee – he thought it was the Golux. 'Come out, you crooning knave!' he cried. 'Stand forward, Zorn of Zorna!'

'He's not here,' said the spy.

They heard the savage clash of swords. 'They've got him!' squealed the Duke. 'Eleven men to one!'

'You may have heard of Galahad,' said Hark, 'whose strength was as the strength of ten.'

'That leaves one man to get him,' cried the Duke. 'I count on Krang, the strongest guard I have, the finest fencer in the world, save one. An unknown prince in armour vanquished him a year ago, somewhere on an island. No one else can do it.'

74

'The unknown prince', said Hark, 'was Zorn of Zorna.'

'I'll slay him then myself!' The Duke's voice rose and echoed down the dark and secret stairs. 'I slew time with the bloody hand that grips your arm, and time is greater far than Zorn of Zorna!'

Hark began to chew again. 'No mortal man can murder time,' he said, 'and even if he could, there's something else: a clockwork in a maiden's heart, that strikes the hours of youth and love, and knows the southward swan from winter snow, and summer afternoons from tulip time.'

'You sicken me with your chocolate chatter,' snarled the Duke. 'Your tongue is made of candy. I'll slay this ragged prince, if Krang has missed him. If there were light, I'd show you on my sleeves the old brown stains of seconds, where they bled and died. I slew time in these gloomy halls, and wiped my bloody blade –'

'Ah, shut up,' said Hark. 'You are the most aggressive villain in the world. I always meant to tell you that. I said it and I'm glad.'

'Silence,' roared the Duke. 'Where are we?' They stumbled down the secret stairs.

'This is the hidden door,' said Hark, 'that leads into the oak room.'

'Open,' roared the Duke, his sword gripped in his hand. Hark groped and found the secret knob.

8

THE black oak room was bright with
flaming torches, but brighter with the
light of Saralinda. The cold eye of the
Duke was dazzled by the gleaming of a thousand
jewels that sparkled on the table. His ears were
filled with chiming as the clocks began to strike.

'One!' said Hark.

'Two!' cried Zorn of Zorna.

'Three!' the Duke's voice almost whispered.

'Four!' sighed Saralinda.

'Five!' the Golux crowed, and pointed at the table. 'The task is done, the terms are met,' he said.

The Duke's cold eye slowly moved around the room. 'Where are my guards?' he croaked, 'and where is Krang, the greatest of them all?'

'I lured them to the tower,' said Zorn, 'and locked them in. The one that's tied in knots is Krang.'

The Duke glared at the jewels on the table. 'They're false!' he said. 'They must be coloured pebbles!' He picked one up, and saw that it was real, and put it down again.

'The task is done,' said Hark, 'the terms are met.'

'Not until I count them,' said the Duke. 'If there be only one that isn't here, I wed the Princess Saralinda on the morrow.' The figures in the room were still and he could hear their breathing.

'What a gruesome way to treat one's niece,' the Golux cried.

'She's not my niece,' the lame man sneered. 'I stole her from a king.' He showed his lower teeth. 'We all have flaws,' he said, 'and mine is being wicked.' He sat down at the table and began to count the gems.

'Who is my father then?' the Princess cried.

The spy's black eyebrows rose. 'I thought the Golux told you, but then, of course, he never could remember things.'

'Especially,' the Golux said, 'the names of kings.'

'Your father', said the spy, 'is good King Gwain of Yarrow.'

'I knew that once,' the Golux said, 'but I forgot it.' He turned to Saralinda. 'Then the gift your father gave to Hagga has operated in the end to make you happy.'

The Duke looked up and bared his teeth. 'The tale is much too tidy for my taste,' he snarled. 'I hate it.' He went on counting.

'It's neat,' said Hark, 'and, to *my* taste, refreshing.' He removed his mask. His eyes were bright and jolly. 'If I may introduce myself,' he said, 'I am a servant of the King, the good King Gwain of Yarrow.'

'That,' the Golux said, 'I didn't know. You could have saved the Princess many years ago.'

The servant of the King looked sad, and said, 'This part I always hate to tell, but I was under a witch's spell.'

'I weary of witches,' the Golux said, 'with due respect to Mother.'

The Duke's smile showed his upper teeth. 'I cannot even trust the spies I see,' he muttered. His eye moved glassily around and saw the Golux. 'You mere Device!' he gnarled. 'You platitude! You Golux *ex machina*!'

'Quiet, please,' the Golux said, 'you gleaming thief.'

'Nine hundred ninety-eight.' The Duke was counting. 'Nine hundred ninety-nine.' He had counted all the jewels, and put them in a sack. There was none left on the table. He gave them all a look of horrid glee. 'The Princess', said the Duke, 'belongs to me.'

A deathly silence filled the room. The Golux turned a little pale and his hand began to shake. He remembered something in the dark, coming down from Hagga's hill, that struck against his

ankle, a sapphire or a ruby that had fallen from the sack. 'One thousand,' groaned the Duke, in a tone of vast surprise. A diamond had fallen from his glove, the left one, and no one but the Golux saw it fall. The Duke stood up and sneered. 'What are you waiting for?' he shrieked. 'Depart! If you be gone forever, it will not be long enough! If you return no more, then it will be too soon!' He slowly turned to Zorn. 'What kind of knots?' he snarled.

'Turk's head,' the young Prince said. 'I learned them from my sister.'

'Begone!' the cold Duke screamed again, and bathed his hands in rubies. 'My jewels', he croaked, 'will last forever.' The Golux, who had never tittered, tittered. The great doors of the oak room opened, and they left the cold Duke standing there, up to his wrists in diamonds.

'Yarrow', said the Prince, 'is half-way on our journey.' They stood outside the castle.

'You'll need these,' said the Golux. He held the reins of two white horses. 'Your ship lies in the harbour. It sails within the hour.'

'It sails at midnight,' Hark corrected him.

'I can't remember everything,' the Golux said. 'My father's clocks were always slow. He also lacked the power of concentration.'

Zorn helped the Princess to her saddle. She gazed a last time at the castle. 'A fair wind stands for Yarrow,' said the Prince.

The Golux gazed a last time at the Princess. 'Keep warm,' he said. 'Ride close together. Remember laughter. You'll need it even in the blessed isles of Ever After.'

'There are no horses in the stables,' mused the Prince. 'Whence came these white ones?'

'The Golux has a lot of friends,' said Hark. 'I guess they give him horses when he needs them. But on the other hand, he may have made them up. He makes things up, you know.'

'I know he does,' sighed Zorn of Zorna. 'You sail for Yarrow with us?'

'I must stay a fortnight longer,' Hark replied. 'So runs my witch's spell. It will give me time to tidy up, and untie Krang as well.'

They looked around for the old Device, but he was there no longer. 'Where has he gone?' cried Saralinda.

'Oh,' said Hark, 'he knows a lot of places.'

'Give him,' Saralinda said, 'my love, and this.'
Hark took the rose.

The two white horses snorted snowy mist in the cool green glade that led down to the harbour. A fair wind stood for Yarrow and, looking far to sea, the Princess Saralinda thought she saw, as people often think they see, on clear and windless days, the distant shining shores of Ever After. Your guess is quite as good as mine (there are a lot of things that shine) but I have always thought she did, and I will always think so.

Epilogue

A FORTNIGHT later, the Duke was gloating over his jewels in the oak room when they suddenly turned to tears, with a little sound like sighing. The fringes of his glowing gloves were stained with Hagga's laughter. He staggered to his feet and drew his sword, and

85

shouted, 'Whisper!' In the courtyard of the castle six startled geese stopped hunting snails and looked up at the oak room. 'What slish is *this*?' exclaimed the Duke, disgusted by the pool of melted gems leering on the table. His monocle fell, and he slashed his sword at silence and at nothing. Something moved across the room, like monkeys and like shadows. The torches on the walls went out, the two clocks stopped, and the room grew colder. There was a smell of old, un-opened rooms and the sound of rabbits scream-ing. 'Come on, you blob of glup,' the cold Duke roared. 'You may frighten octopi to death, you gibbous spawn of hate and thunder, but not the Duke of Coffin Castle!' He sneered. 'Now that my precious gems have turned to thlup, living on, alone and cold, is not my fondest wish! On guard, you musty sofa!' The Todal gleeped. There was a stifled shriek and silence.

When Hark came into the room, holding a lighted lantern above his head, there was no one there. The Duke's sword lay gleaming on the floor, and from the table dripped the jewels of Hagga's laughter, that never last forever, like the jewels of sorrow, but turn again to tears a fortnight after. Hark stepped on something that squtched beneath his foot and flobbed against the wall. He picked it up and held it near the lantern. It was the small black ball stamped with scarlet owls. The last spy of the Duke of Coffin Castle, alone and lonely in the gloomy room, thought he heard, from somewhere far away, the sound of someone laughing.

The Wonderful

*For Ted Gardiner
and his Julias and Patricias,
with love and other
good O words*

I

SOMEWHERE a ponderous tower clock slowly
dropped a dozen strokes into the gloom.
Storm clouds rode low along the horizon,
and no moon shone. Only a melancholy chorus
of frogs broke the soundlessness. Then a strange
figure appeared out of the nocturnal somno-

lence, as unexpectedly as the blare of a bugle in a lullaby. He entered the tavern near the sea, and a blade of light flashed into the blackness and disappeared when the old oaken door closed once more.

The newcomer was a seafaring man, and the sight of him turned the taverners silent. There was a green parrot on the man's shoulder, and a tarred pigtail hung down his back. He carried no crutch, for he had two legs, and he rolled like a goose when he walked. His voice when he spoke was as deep as a gong in a tomb.

'Call me Littlejack!' he roared, and the taverners called him Littlejack.

A lean, silent man at a shadowy table in a corner, wearing a black cape and black gloves, beckoned to the newcomer, who sat down across from him. 'You look like a man with a map,' whispered the man in black.

'I am a man with a map,' boomed Littlejack. 'It is a map of a far and lonely island, rich with jewels, sapphires, emeralds, and rubies. I seek a man with a ship.'

'I am a man with a ship,' said the man in black.

'And a crew to man her?'

'And a crew to man her.'

'Are you a man with a name?' asked Littlejack.

'I am a man named Black,' said the man named Black. They shook hands, one heavy and bare, the other thin and gloved, and reached a bargain at one o'clock: 'Two-thirds of the booty for me and you, the other third will go to the crew.'

Black smiled, and when he smiled he showed his lower teeth. 'Now let me see the map,' he said. And he took the map and studied it. 'There are no crosses here,' said Black, 'or marks. There should be crosses here and marks, indicating where the jewels lie hidden.'

'There is another map with marks and crosses, but what became of it and where it is, no man can say,' said Littlejack.

'We'll find the map, or if we don't, we'll find the jewels without it,' Black declared. He gazed at Littlejack as if the sailor were a jigsaw puzzle that had too many parts, or not enough. 'You have the mien and manner of a man out of the past. Where do you come from?'

The sailor grinned. 'Not, matey, from the regions which are wholly land. I'll take the map.'

'It's safe with me,' said Black.

'It's safer if we cut the thing in two,' said Little-jack. And with his cutlass he cut the map in two. And Black took half of it and Littlejack the other half.

They went aboard the ship at two o'clock. 'I can't make out her name,' said Littlejack. 'How is she called?'

'The *Aeiu*,' said Black.

'A weird, uncanny name,' the sailor said. 'It sounds a little like a night bird screaming.'

'It's all the vowels except the O,' Black said. 'I've had a hatred of that letter ever since the night my mother became wedged in a porthole. We couldn't pull her in and so we had to push her out.' He shuddered and his eyes turned hard. 'What is the name of this island?' he asked, shaking off the thought of O.

'Ooroo,' said Littlejack, and once more the other shuddered.

'I hate the name,' he said at last. 'It sounds like the eyes of a couple of ghosts leaning against an R. I speak O-words myself, so I can spit them out.' Something screamed. 'A night bird,' whispered Black. 'The sailors say it's my mother. Let's go below. I've got a cabin full of rum.'

2

WHEN the dawn came up the *Aeiu*, whose
sails were black as raven wings, could no
longer be seen from shore, even by the
sharpest eye and strongest glass. The weather was
fair and the voyage was long. Then early one
morning the ship came into the only port of the

far and lonely island, and Black and Littlejack went ashore, the former softly, and the latter swaggering, followed by their surly and sinewy crew.

'We have come for your jewels,' Black told a spokesman of the quiet people, 'with cutlasses and pistols.'

'With axes and spades and cudgels,' said Littlejack.

'We have no jewels,' said the spokesman, 'except the blue of the water, and the pink of our maidens' cheeks and lips, and the green of our fields.'

'We have come for your jewels,' repeated Black.

'We have only moonstones and opals, and other ordinary stones,' the spokesman said.

'Ordinary stones, ordinary stones!' squawked the green parrot.

'There is a map,' said Black, 'a secret map, with marks and crosses, indicating where the jewels lie hidden.'

'I know of no such map,' the spokesman said.

Black grinned and showed his lower teeth

again. 'Take the town apart,' he cried, and the crew began taking the town apart, with axes and spades and cudgels, smashing the locks off doors, prying the lids from boxes, breaking into closets and cupboards, but all they found was moonstones and opals and other ordinary stones, lockets and love-notes, options, contracts, mortgages, records, reports, and other documents, but neither precious stones nor any map.

'Dig in the woods,' commanded Black.

'Dig in the meadows,' ordered Littlejack. And the crew dug in the woods and in the meadows, but all they found was owls in oaks, moss and moles, toads and toadstools, roots and rocks.

'Drain the brooks,' snarled Black.

'Drain the pools,' roared Littlejack. And the crew drained the brooks and the pools, but all they found was trout and tortoises, frogs and worms, and an owl that had drowned in a pool.

'Owls in oaks, owls in pools!' squawked the parrot.

The crew then turned to towers and fountains with their axes and cudgels, but all they got for their sweat and pains was the stones that towers are built of, and the sparkle of fountain water.

That night Black and Littlejack sat at a table in a tavern, drinking rum from tankards. 'There must be sapphires,' whispered Black.

'And emeralds and rubies,' grumbled Littlejack.

'Opals and moonstones,' squawked the parrot. 'Love-notes, lockets, options. Owls in oaks, moss and moles, and mortgages.'

'Stop his squawking,' Black exclaimed, 'or else I'll squck his thrug till all he can whupple is geep.'

'All he can whupple is geep, all he can whupple is geep,' squawked the parrot.

'Still, I'm glad he named the things we found,' said Black, after a moment. 'Everything we find has an O in its name, and everywhere we look has an O in its name, and everything we open – closets, cupboards, woods, meadows.'

'Floors and roofs,' added Littlejack, 'and brooks and pools.'

Black stared into his tankard, while the tavern clock ticked sixty times. 'I hate things with an O in their names,' cried Black. 'That goes for clocks and parrots.' He threw his tankard at the clock and broke it open, but there was nothing inside but works, no rubies, no emeralds, and no sapphires, and no map.

'The parrot's name's Magraw,' said Littlejack. 'There ain't no O in that.'

'Squck his thrug,' squawked the parrot. 'Squck his thrug.'

'And there ain't no O in that,' said Littlejack.

Black stood up and smote the table with his fist. 'I'll get rid of O, in upper case and lower,' cried the man in black. 'I'll issue an edict. All words in books or signs with an O in them shall have the O erased or painted out. We'll print new books and paint new signs without an O in them.'

And so the locksmith became a lcksmith, and the bootmaker a btmaker, and people whispered like conspirators when they said the names. *Love's Labour's Lost* and *Mother Goose* flattened out like a pricked balloon. Books were bks and Robinhood was Rbinhd. Little Goody Two Shoes lost her O's and so did Goldilocks, and the former became a whisper, and the latter sounded like a key jiggled in a lck. It was impossible to read 'cockadoodledoo' aloud, and parents gave up reading to their children, and some gave up reading altogether, and the search for the precious jewels went on.

The afternoon after the night at the tavern, while O's were being taken out of books and out of signs, so that the cw jumped over the mn, and the dish ran away with the spn, and the clockshop became a clckshp, the toymaker a tymaker, Black issued new searching orders. 'Look in violins and cellos,' he commanded.

'Look in trombones, horns, and oboes,' thundered Littlejack. And the crew looked in violins and cellos, trombones, horns, and oboes, piccolos and banjos, finding nothing, for nothing came out of them except music.

That night in the tavern, after his thirteenth pint of rum, Black began to sing a ditty in a voice that had the timbre of a buzzard's:

'I won't go down the horrible street
  To see the horrible people.
I'll gladly climb the terrible stair
  That leads to the terrible steeple
And the terrible bats, and the terrible rats,
  And the cats in the terrible steeple.
But I won't go down the horrible street
  To see the horrible people.'

As he sang, the taverners stared at him and then they left their drinks unfinished, paid for them, and slunk away into the night.

'Methinks the people have a loathing for your voice and for your song,' said Littlejack.

'I'll take away from them', said Black, 'everything that plays and has an O.'

And so the following morning the crew went from house to house, seizing violins and cellos, trombones, horns, and oboes, pianos, harpsichords and clavichords, accordions and melodeons, bassoons and saxophones, and all the other instruments with O's, up to and including the woodwinds. A man and his wife who loved to play duets on mandolin and glockenspiel drifted apart. Children, forbidden the use of combs, could no longer play tunes on combs with tissue paper. The crew spent the afternoon breaking up an old calliope they had found rusting in a field, and taking apart a carillon.

'All they have is fifes and drums and cymbals,' gloated Black.

'And zithers and guitars,' said Littlejack. 'And dulcimers and spinets, and bugles, harps, and trumpets.'

'Much good they'll get from these,' said Black, 'or any others. I haven't finished with the O's in music, in harmony and melody, that is, and compositions. They'll have no score, and what is more, no orchestra, or podium, or baton, and no conductor. They can't play symphonies, or rhapsodies, sonatas or concerti. I'll take away their oratorios and choirs and choruses, and all their soloists, their baritones and tenors and sopranos, their altos and contraltos and accompanists. All they'll have is the funeral march, the chant and anthem, and the dirge, and certain snatches.'

'They'll still have serenades,' said Littlejack.

Black made an evil and impatient gesture. 'You can't serenade a lady on a balcony,' he said, 'if there isn't any balcony. Let them hum their hymns and lisp their litanies.' Black's eyes began to glow as he named O-names that would have to go: 'Scherzo, largo, and crescendo, allegro and diminuendo. Let the lyric writers have their Night in June. Much good it'll do 'em without the moon.' He crushed an imaginary moon in his hand. 'At least the people cannot dance the polka, or the schottische, or gavotte. I wish they mourned their loss, here on R, but they do not.'

'R?' asked Littlejack.

'I've taken the O's out of Ooroo,' Black explained. 'Isles with O's in their names are few, and invariably unlucky, such as the Isle of Lyonesse, which sank into the sea. I've made a list of isles still standing, none of which has a trace of O. It must mean something.' He pulled a parchment from his pocket and read the names of O-less isles aloud: 'Iceland, Greenland, England, Wales, and Ireland; Jersey, Guernsey, Man, and Wight; Capri, Crete, and Cyprus; Elba, Malta, and St Helena; Madagascar, Zanzibar, Sardinia –'

'St Helena and Elba', said Littlejack, 'were not too lucky for Napoleon.'

'Napoleon Bonaparte,' said Black, 'was born on Corsica. His bad luck started there.' And then he resumed the reading of his list: 'Bali and the Baleares, the Philippines and Celebes, the Fijis and the Hebrides, Cuba and Bermuda, the East Indies and West Indies, the Lesser and the Greater Antilles, Martinique and Trinidad, Easter and Jamaica, the Virgins and Canaries, Sicily and Haiti and Hawaii. And add a T to Haiti for

Tahiti.' His voice gave out before the list was finished.

Littlejack, closed one eye and said, 'You left out one. A friend of mine named Gunn lived there, if you could call it living.'

'Its name', breathed Black, 'is Treasure.'

3

THAT night the people of the town and those who lived in the country met secretly in the woods. They had been called together by a poet named Andreus, who read aloud, or tried to read, a poem he had just had printed at the printer's. It was called *The Mn*

Belngs T Lvers, but the poetry had died in it with the death of its O's. 'Soon Black and Littlejack', said Andreus, 'will no longer let us live in houses, for houses have an O.'

'Or cottages,' said the blacksmith, 'for cottage has an O, and so does bungalow.'

'We'll have to live in huts,' the baker said, 'or shacks, or sheds, or shanties, or in cabins.'

'Cabins without logs,' said Andreus. 'We shall have mantels but no clocks, shelves without crocks, keys without locks, walls without doors, rugs without floors, frames without windows, chimneys with no roofs to put them on, knives without a fork or spoon, beds without pillows. There will be no wood for our fires, no oil for our lamps, and no hobs for our kettles.'

'They will take my dough,' moaned the baker.

'They will take my gold,' moaned the gold-smith.

'And my forge,' sighed the blacksmith.

'And my cloth,' wept the tailor.

'And my chocolate,' muttered the candymaker.

At this a man named Hyde arose and spoke. 'Chocolate is bad for the stomach,' he said. 'We shall still have wintergreen and peppermint. Hail to Black and Littlejack, who will liberate us all from liquorice and horehound!'

'Hyde is a lawyer,' Andreus pointed out, 'and he will still have his fees and fines.'

'And his quills and ink,' said the baker.

'And his paper and parchment,' said the goldsmith.

'And his chair and desk,' said the blacksmith.

'And his signs and seals,' said the tailor.

'And his briefs and liens,' said the candymaker.

But the lawyer waved them all aside. 'We shall all have an equal lack of opportunity,' he said smoothly. 'We shall all have the same amount of nothing. There must be precious jewels, or Black and Littlejack would not have come so far to search for them. I suggest we look in nooks and corners and in pigeon-holes ourselves.' Some of the men agreed with Hyde, but most of them took the poet's side.

'We must think of a way to save our homes,' the poet said. And they sat on the ground until the moon went down, trying to think of a way. And even as they thought, Black and Littlejack and their men were busily breaking open dolls, and yellow croquet balls, and coconuts, but all they found was what is always found in dolls, and yellow croquet balls, and coconuts.

The next morning Andreus was walking with his poodle in a street whose cobblestones had been torn up in the search for jewels when he encountered Black and Littlejack.

'You are *both* pets now,' sneered Littlejack, 'for the O has gone out of poet, and out of trochee and strophe and spondee, and ode and sonnet and rondeau.'

The poodle growled.

'I hate poodles,' snarled Black, 'for poodles have a double O.'

'My pet is French,' said Andreus. 'He is not only a *chien*, which is French for dog, but a *caniche*, which is French for poodle.'

'*Chien caniche*,' squawked the parrot. '*Chien caniche*.'

'Then I will get rid of the other domestic creatures with an O,' cried Black, and he issued an edict to this effect.

There was great consternation on the island now, for people could have pigs, but no hogs or pork or bacon; sheep, but no mutton or wool; calves, but no cows. Geese were safe as long as

one of them did not stray from the rest and become a goose, and if one of a family of mice wandered from the nest, he became a mouse and lost
his impunity. Children lost their ponies, and
farmers their colts and horses and goats and their
donkeys and their oxen.

Test cases were constantly brought to court –
or curt, as it was called. 'Somebody will have to
clarify the law for everybody, or nobody will
know where anybody stands,' the people said. So
Black appointed Hyde lawyer, judge, and chief
clarifier. 'The more chaotic the clarification,' said
Black, 'the better. Remember how I hate that
letter.'

This was right up Hyde's dark and devious
alley. 'Chaotic is now chatic,' he said, 'a cross between chaos and static.' He decided that farmers
could keep their cows if they kept them in herds,
for cows in herds are kine or cattle. And so the
people had milk and cheese and butter. He decided in favour of hens and eggs, if hens were
segregated. 'Keep them out of flocks,' he said,
'for flocks are not only flocks, but also poultry.'

'We have no corn or potatoes, or cauliflower,
or tomatoes,' a housewife said one day.

'In a vegetable garden,' said Hyde, 'the things that grow are ninety-five per cent without an O. I could name you twenty such,' he added cockily, 'and then you'd scream in unison for broccoli. Almost all the fruits are yours to eat, from the apple to the tangerine, with a good two dozen in between. I'll stick to those that start with P to show you what I mean: the pear, the peach, the plum, the prune, the plantain and pineapple, the pawpaw and papaya. But you will yearn for things you never ate, and cannot tolerate – I know you women – the pomegranate, for one, and the dull persimmon. No grapefruit, by the way. I hate its bitter juice. I have banned it, under its French name, *pamplemousse*.'

Another wife took the stand one day to complain of the things she hadn't. 'Cloves and cinnamon,' she said, 'and marjoram and saffron.'

'You still have dill,' said Hyde, 'and thyme and sage and basil, vinegar, vanilla, and sarsaparilla, salt and pepper and paprika, ginger and the spices. You can't have coffee, but there is tea; to sweeten it, there's sugar.'

A seamstress raised her hand to ask about the O's in textiles, fabrics, and in clothes. 'You're denied a few,' admitted Hyde. 'Corduroy and bombazine, organdy and tricotine, calico and crinoline. But you have silk and satin, velvet, lace and linen, tulle and twill and tweed, damask and denim, madras and muslin, felt and chintz and baize and leather, and twenty more for cool and warm and winter weather.'

Now the boatswain of the crew was a man named Stragg and the cockswain was a man named Strugg, and the former was allergic to roses, and the latter was allergic to phlox. So Black decided that even the flowers with an O in their names were against him, and he ordered his crew to get rid of roses and phlox in the gardens of the island, and oleanders and moonflowers and morning-glories, and cosmos and coxcomb and columbine, and all the rest with O's.

'But my livelihood is violets and hollyhocks and marigolds,' a gardener complained.

'Lilies are nice for livelihood,' said Hyde, 'and more alliterative. There are also lilacs and the like. I crossbreed certain things myself with more success than failure. Forget-me-nots, when crossed with madwort, lose their O's. I get a hybrid which I call regret-me-evers. Love-in-a-mist, when crossed with bleeding hearts, results in sweet-hearts quarrels.'

'It's blasphemy or heresy,' the women cried, 'or something!'

'You haven't heard the half of it,' said Hyde. 'Black-eyed susans, crossed with ragged sailors, give me ragged susans. Jack-in-the-pulpit, crossed with devil's paintbrush, should give me devil-in-the-pulpit. And think of the fine satanic chimes that will emerge from hellebore crossed with Canterbury bells.' At this the women rose in anger and dismay and left the curt without a curtsy.

'Why not get rid of all the flowers?' demanded Black one day. 'After all, there is an O in flowers.'

'I thought of that,' said Hyde, 'but we must spare collective nouns, like food, and goods, and crops, and tools, and, I should think, the lesser schools. I have taken the carpenter's gouge and boards. It still leaves him much too much, but that's the way it goes, with and without O's. He has his saw and axe and hatchet, his hammer and chisel, his brace and bit, and plane and level, also nails and tacks and brads and screws and staples. But all he can build is bric-a-brac and knickknack, gew-gaw, kickshaw, and gimcrack. No coop or goathouse, no stoop or boathouse.'

'I would that I could banish body; then I'd get rid of everybody.' Black's eyes gleamed like rubies. 'No more anatomy, and no morphology, physiognomy, or physiology, or people, or even persons. I think about it often in the night. Body is blood and bones and other O's, organs, torso, abdomen, and toes.'

Hyde curled his upper lip. 'I'll build you a better man,' he said, 'of firmer flesh and all complete, from hairy head to metatarsal feet, using A's and I's and U's and E's, with muscular arms and flexible knees; eyes and ears and lids and lips, neck and chest and breast and hips; liver, heart, and lungs and chin, nerves and ligaments and skin; kidneys, pancreas, and flanks, ankles, calves, and shins and shanks; legs and lashes, ribs and spleen –' Black had turned a little green, and then Hyde held up both his hands. 'Brains and veins and cells and glands –'

'Silence!' thundered Black. 'I wish that more things had an O.'

Hyde sighed. 'There is no O in everything,' he said. 'We can't change that.'

'I will not take their vocal chords, or tongues, or throats,' said Black, 'but I shall make these jewel-hiders speak without the use of O in any word they say.'

And so language and the spoken word diminished and declined as the people were forced to speak without the use of O in any word. No longer could the people say Heigh-Ho, Yoohoo, or Yo ho ho, or even plain Hello. The theatre in the town was closed, for Shakespeare's lines without an O sound flat and muffled. No one could play *Othello* when *Othello* turned to *Thell*, and Desdemona was strangled at the start. Some sentences became so strange they sounded like a foreign tongue. 'Dius gre gling minus gress' meant 'Odious ogre ogling ominous ogress', but only scholars knew it. Spoken words became a hissing and a mumble, or a murmur and a hum. A man named Otto Ott, when asked his name, could only stutter. Ophelia Oliver repeated hers, and vanished from the haunts of men.

'We can't tell shot from shoot, or hot from hoot,' the blacksmith said, in secret meeting with his fellows.

'We can't tell rot from root, or owed from wed,' the baker said.

'It's even worse than that,' said Andreus, 'for oft becomes the same as foot, and odd the same as dodo. Something must be done at once, or we shall never know what we are saying.' And he was right. Some people said that moles were mulls, while others called them emmels. The author of a book called *Flamingo Stories* read *Flaming Stries* aloud to his wife, and gave up writing.

'I still hear laughter,' Black complained to Hyde one day. 'After all I've done to them I still hear laughter.'

'There is no O in laughter,' Hyde reminded him, 'or in smile, or grin, or giggle. There is, of course, an O in chortle, but none in chuckle or in snicker.'

'Don't play games with me!' snarled Black. 'Games,' he repeated, chewing the word as if it were candy. 'Take their yo-yos and diavolos and dominoes; throw their quoits and shuttlecocks away, and everything pertaining to croquet; shuffleboard and crochinole must go, Post Office, pillow, and ticktacktoe. Ping-pong –'

Hyde raised his hand in quick dissent. 'Table

tennis', he said, 'is played with O-less paddles, balls, and net, upon an O-less table.'

Black went on naming the names of what were now illegal games. 'Let them play tiddlywinks', said Black, 'and mumblety-peg.'

Hyde recruited a dozen men, and soon a dozen others were helping them to keep the people from playing certain games at night in cellars – leapfrog, hopscotch, and Pussy Wants a Corner.

'We live in peril and in danger,' Andreus told the people, 'and in a little time may have left few things that we can say. Already there is little we can play. I have a piece that I shall read. It indicates the quandary we're in.' And then he read it:

'They are swing chas. What is slid? What is left that's slace? We are begne and webegne. Life is bring and brish. Even schling is flish. Animals in the z are less lacnic than we. Vices are filled with paths and scial intercurse is baths. Let us gird up ur lins like lins and rt the hrrr and ust the afs.'

'What nannibickering is this?' cried the blacksmith. 'What is this gibberish?'

'English,' said Andreus, 'without its O's.' And he read the piece again with all its O's and double

O's. Many had figured webegne was woebegone, but none could tell that begne was obegone.

'How shall we dispel this nightmare of flishness?' demanded the baker, who could not say f for of.

'The answer must lie', said Andreus, 'in what has been written. I suggest that we all read what we have left in libraries, searching the secret, hunting the scheme and spell that may bring an end to Black and Littlejack.'

It was dark in the woods that night, and Andreus and his followers did not realize that Hyde listened to their plans, concealed behind a tree. He had been barred from bar and meetings by his colleagues and his countrymen. The next morning the outlawed lawyer went to Black and told what he had heard.

'Destroy all books that might be helpful,' commanded Black, 'especially those dealing with studies and sciences that have O's in their names: geography, biography, biology, psychology, philosophy, philology, astronomy, agronomy, gastronomy, trigonometry, geometry, optometry, and all the other ologies and onomies and ometries.'

The crew set about their new task with a will, and before they were through they had torn down colleges and destroyed many a book and tome and volume, and globe and blackboard and pointer, and banished professors, assistant professors, scholars, tutors, and instructors. There was no one left to translate English into English. Babies often made as much sense as their fathers.

4

THERE walked in beauty on the island a maiden named Andrea. In her father's library one night, searching for the secret and the spell that might confound the vandals and in the end get rid of them, she found an ancient book of magic. The next night Andrea brought the book to the secret meeting in the woods. Andreus was fearful, for women had not been permitted to take part in the meetings. The poet was afraid that women might be banished from the island because of the O in women and in woman.

'They would banish mothers, too,' said Andreus, forgetting to speak in words without an O.

'A maiden is safe as a maiden,' Andrea pointed out, 'and as a lass, or girl, or damsel, and as virgin, and as spinster.'

'And as a darling and a dear,' said Andreus. 'But still you are a woman.'

'I could become a bride and wife,' said Andrea. 'Bride and wife are more than woman.'

'Then you would be a matron,' said Andreus, 'without the hope of tot or toddler, boy or moppet.'

'Enough of this puppybabble and pussyfret,' the wheelwright whined. 'I have no spokes for my wheels, and wheels without spokes are like words without O's.'

'I have no tallow for my candles,' complained the candlemaker, 'and candles without tallow are not candles.'

'Be not afraid to speak with O's,' said Andrea

at last. 'We cannot live or speak without hope, and hope without its O is nothing, and even nothing is less than nothing when it is nthing. Hope contains the longest O of all. We mustn't lose it.' Thereupon she gave Andreus the book she had found in her father's library.

'It is called *The Enchanted Castle*,' said Andreus.

'I know the book,' quavered an old man with a white beard, 'and I can tell you what it says, and spare you the time and trouble of reading a book aloud that has no O's in any word.'

'Then tell us what it says,' cried Andreus, 'for it is full of footnotes which are now called ftntes.'

The old man cleared his throat and spoke. 'Listen, my children, and you shall hear of a magical castle which will appear one month from tonight in this very year.' And he told the tale of the enchanted castle, while the others listened in silence. 'There was a king upon this island once, a thousand years ago, but he was driven from his castle by such a crew of bashlocks and shatterclocks as plagues us now. They took the castle apart and down, stone by stone, searching for precious jewels or a map which were not there, or, if they were, could not be found. The king was banished from the island, but as he left he put a wondrous spell upon the ground where once the castle stood.' The old man stopped to scratch his head.

'How runs this spell?' demanded Andreus.

'Perhaps the maiden here remembers. My memory is no longer what it was,' the old man said.

'Every hundred years the castle shall appear again,' Andrea said, 'in semblance and in seeming, an enchanted castle, such as children see when they are dreaming.'

'And who may enter there?' asked Andreus. 'And why and wherefore?'

Andrea raised her hands and let them fall. 'The last page of the book is lost,' she said.

'The last page of the book contained a map,' the old man murmured. 'My memory isn't what it was, but I remember that.' He stood awhile in silence, then went on. 'Whoever finds the map will find a jewel in everything he opens. My memory isn't what it was, but I remember that.'

'Where is this map?' asked Andreus. 'Can you remember that?'

The old man thought and thought before he spoke. 'It's on a wall, I seem to recall, an old wall in the castle. Whoever finds it will find a certain jewel without which men are lost.'

'Then we shall be first upon the scene when the castle reappears,' cried Andreus.

The old man shook his head in gloom. 'Only evil men may enter there,' he said. 'So runs the royal spell. I know not why, and if I ever knew, I have forgotten.'

'Then we are lost,' said Andreus.

'We can't be lost when lost has lost its O,' the old man said. 'Or can we?'

The others turned away lest they reveal the look of doom upon their faces. The old man spoke again. 'I seem to hear a strange new bell, an old familiar bell, a bell I never heard before, a bell that I remember.'

The others turned to him and stared. And in the gloom Andrea whispered, 'A bell of triumph, or a knell?'

'Time', the old man sighed, 'will tell.'

5

THE vandals spent the next day breaking into
cupolas and cracking open cornices and
cornerstones, smashing gargoyles into bits,
and razing marble columns, Ionic, Doric, Gothic,
and Corinthian, and everything baroque or rococo.
In one cool, cloistered corridor Black himself

smashed with an axe marble busts of Homer and Horace and Plato, Ovid and Omar and Cato, Diogenes and Damocles, Socrates and Hippocrates, and Demosthenes and Aristophanes. Not a single sparkle sparkled in the rubble.

'Why don't we open tombs?' Littlejack inquired one day. 'Jewels are often hid in tombs.'

'Tombs are in cemeteries,' Black replied. 'I have come to hold a great respect for words that have no O. That is why we shall invade no shrine, or church, or chapel.'

'Perhaps you have a certain dread of ghosts and ghouls,' said Littlejack. 'They howl in O, you know, and so do goblins and hobgoblins. But spooks and phantoms have an O we cannot touch.'

'I hate all O's I cannot touch,' Black muttered with a shudder.

'The alphabet has taken over,' Littlejack complained. 'What was the letter of the law is now the law of the letter.'

'None the less, we search no place without an O,' said Black. 'That is why I've left untouched the jungle and the desert and the swamp, the wilderness and wasteland. Besides, they're full of animals with A and E and I and U in all their names: the camel and the elephant, the aardvark and the platypus, the yak, the zebra and the gnu, the tiger and the jaguar, the panther and the puma and the lynx. I have a certain liking now for creatures of this kind.'

'*I* have a certain fear of animals with O,' said Littlejack, 'I know not why.'

'I happen to know there are no animals with O,' said Black. 'I'll tell you why. There is a man named Filch among the crew.'

'A sticky-fingered lad,' said Littlejack.

'Whose sticky fingers found an ancient document somewhere among the ruins we have made,' said Black.

'How goes this document?' asked Littlejack.

Black showed his lower teeth. 'It tells of how a king in olden times, whose niece was bitten by a crocodile, banished all the larger animals with O from desert, swamp, and jungle – the crocodile, the lion, and the boar, the python and the cobra and the boa, the gorilla and the gibbon and the wolf. Orang-utans and baboons disappeared. The porcupine, the mongoose, and the sloth, the dingo and the leopard and the potto were driven from their tree, or cave, or grotto.'

'The rhinoceros and the hippopotamus?' asked Littlejack.

'Gone with the otter and the kangaroo,' said Black. 'There are no creatures left with O here on this island, except a few so small they cannot plague us.' And once again that night he said, seated in the tavern, 'There are no animals with O to plague us.'

A barmaid heard his words, and when her work was done she joined the others at their secret meeting in the woods and told them all what Black had said. And at this moment Hyde appeared among them, as if from nowhere. 'Your furred and finned and feathered friends with O are either gone, or quite extinct, or never were!' he cried. 'The dinosaur and the brontosaurus, the mammoth and the behemoth, old ichthyosaurus and the pterodactyl, the dodo and the mastodon.' He turned to Andreus and said sarcastically, 'The only other animals with O are mythical. Why don't you call on them for help?'

'What animals are these that never were?' the old man asked. 'My memory isn't what it was, you know. I find it very hard to think of things that haven't been.'

'The unicorn, the dragon, and the Minotaur,' said Hyde, 'demons out of legend and of lore – the griffon and the cockatrice, the Phoenix and the Gorgon and the roc, the ogo-pogo and the monster in the Loch. And if these ten don't make a quorum, why, call upon the cockalorum.' The moon had gone behind a cloud and the people felt cold and fearful, as if they had lost, somehow, their only allies. 'The animals with A and E and I and U are on the side of Black and Littlejack,' said Hyde, 'and that is all there are. Unless, of course, you count the creatures with an O one finds in fairy tales and fantasies – the tove, the mome rath, and the borogrove, the whiffen-poof and wogglebug and Dong, the Pod, the Todal, and the gorm.'

'I never heard of gorms', the old man said, 'or Todals.'

'That's because they never were,' said Hyde, 'except in books, where they are not your friend but foe, since each of them has lost its O.' He left the group and disappeared among the trees, and they could hear his mocking laughter as he went.

Andrea had fallen silent, but now she spoke as if reciting something: 'There are four words with O. You mustn't lose them. Find out what they are and learn to use them.'

'Hope is one,' said Andreus.

'And love,' said Andrea.

'And valour, I should think,' the old man said. And then they tried to find the fourth, naming courage, thought, and reason, devotion, work, and worship.

'None of these is right,' said Andrea. 'I'll know it when I hear it.' And so, until the setting of the moon, they tried out words with O – imagination and religion, dedication and decision, honour, progeny, and vision. 'None of these is the word,' said Andrea. 'I'll know it when I hear it.'

'I hope,' the old man said, 'we think of it in time. Perhaps the word is wisdom.'

'An austere word,' Andrea said, 'but surely not the greatest.' And they spent the rest of the night searching for the greatest, trying youth and joy and jubilation, victory and exaltation, languor, comfort, relaxation, money, fortune, non-taxation, motherhood and domesticity, and many anotherhood and icity. But Andrea shook her

lovely head at every word the people said, reject-
ing soul and contemplation, dismissing courtship
and elation, and many anothership and ation.

'I miss the O', the old man said, 'in faith and
truth and beauty. The O belongs, alas, to lost and
gone, forsaken and forgotten.' The others felt for-
lorn at this, but still the search continued, in all
the hopes and dreams of men, from action to
euphoria. The old man stroked his beard and said,
'*Sic transit verbi gloria*.'

There still were those who spoke with O's, and
one of these was a boatwright, a man of force and
gusto. 'You are still my spouse and not my
spuse,' he told his fearful wife, 'and this is my
house and not my huse, and I make boats, not
bats, and I wear coats, not cats. What', he asked
his youngest son, 'did you learn today in school?'

'It's schl,' his son replied.

'Never hiss at me,' his father cried. 'When I
want aloes, I don't want ales, I hate such names.
And cameos are cameos, not cames. Yesterday I
met a man who wanted four canoes –'

'Fur canes,' his son put in.

'Silence!' his father shouted. 'What did you
learn today in school?'

'That mist is always mist, but what is mist isn't always mist,' his son recited.

At this his father rose up like a storm, put on his hat and cat, and stalked to where the door had been, and reached for where the knob once was.

'Where are yu ging?' whispered his anxious wife.

'Ut!' the boatwright cried, and ut he went.

'What did yu say t yur father that made him leave the huse?' the mother asked her son.

'Mist is always moist,' the boy replied in whispers, 'but what is moist isn't always mist.'

And other odd occurrences occurred. A swain who praised his sweetheart's thrat, and said she sang like a chir of riles or a chrus of vires, was slapped. And so it went, and some lads lost their lasses, and most men lost their tempers, and all men lost their patience, and a few men lost their minds.

Then Black called Hyde one day in consultation. 'Some of the people salute me as I pass,' he growled. 'Do you know why?'

'O-lessness is now a kind of cult in certain quarters,' Hyde observed, 'a messy lessness, whose meaninglessness none the less attracts the few, first one or two, then three or four, then more and more. People often have respect for what they cannot comprehend, since some men cannot always tell their crosses from their blessings, their laurels from their thorns. It shows up in the games they still can play. Charades are far more work than fun, and so are Blind Man's Buff and Hide-and-Seek, and Run, Sheep, Run. O-lessism may become the ism of the future, and men from far and wide, pilgrims on a pilgrimage, may lay their tributes on your grave.'

Black showed his teeth and made a restless gesture. 'Taking a single letter from the alphabet', he said, 'should make life simpler.'

'I don't see why. Take the F from life and you have lie. It's adding a letter to simple that makes it simpler. Taking a letter from hoarder makes it harder.' With a small shrug and a little leer, Hyde turned on his heel and walked away.

Black watched him go and scowled. 'He's much too smart', he said aloud, 'for his own good and for mine.'

6

THERE were no clocks to mark the passing hours, for Black had smashed them all. It was October now, but no one knew what day, for Black had torn from all the calendars the months with O's, October and November. Little enough was left upright, unbroken, or unravaged, and the town without its towers, and the countryside without its fountains and its pools, and the woods which had lost their oaks and hemlocks seemed deserted. The robins and the orioles had gone, and even the whippoorwill no longer sang. Then came the night the old man had predicted.

Black and Littlejack were at their table in the tavern when they heard a hue and cry, and children calling. Dogs without an O, the beagles, bassets, and the spaniels, set up a mournful howling. A wondrous light filled all the sky.

'What revelry is this?' demanded Black.

'I know not what,' said Littlejack, 'but I don't like it.'

'I don't like it, I don't like it,' squawked the parrot, and Black squcked his thrug till all he could whupple was geep.

'Geep,' whuppled the parrot.

Black and Littlejack strode to where the door had been, walking on earth because the floor was gone, and stared up towards the sky. An enormous castle, lighted as by the light of many moons, stood upon a hill a mile away.

'A castle!' cried Black. He rubbed his gloves

together and he gloated. 'The jewels!' he cried. 'The emeralds, the rubies, and the sapphires!'

'Not so fast,' warned Littlejack.

'Faster!' cried Black, and he hurried through the night, stumbling on the torn-up cobbles of the streets, his shining eyes upon the shining castle.

'Not so fast,' warned Littlejack again. 'I smell the smell of trickery and ruse.'

'I smell the smell of jewels,' Black exclaimed. 'I smell a map.'

Their crew had gathered round them now with their axes and their spades and their cudgels, yelping like a pack of hungry hounds, and they all surged towards the castle, urged on by Stragg and Strugg.

From where they stood in the shadow of a broken column, Andreus and Andrea watched them go. 'This is their wildest night, and I hope it is their last,' breathed Andreus.

'Keep saying hope,' the old man said, appearing out of nowhere, 'for we shall need it.'

'There is a footnote in the book', said Andrea, 'which I forgot to mention.'

'How does it read?' asked Andreus.

'That if the men who seek their heart's desire within the castle find it not before the hour of noon tomorrow, their cause is lost.'

'It gives them two long hours and ten, and they must have a hundred men,' said Andreus.

'I could find a map in half that time and all alone,' another man said, 'if I were young.'

'The map is not their heart's desire; it is the jewels,' said Andrea. 'And there is something in the book about a vast frustrating forest.'

'How goes that part?' asked Andreus.

'It was written all in O, or nearly so, and all the O's are gone,' said Andrea. 'When coat is cat, and boat is bat, and goatherd looks like gathered, and booth is both, since both are bth, the reader's eye is bothered.'

'And power is pwer, and zero zer, and, worst of all, a hero's her.' The old man sighed as he said it.

'Anon is ann, and moan is man.' Andrea smiled as she said it.

'And shoe', Andreus said, 'is she.'

'Ah, woe', the old man said, 'is we.'

7

BLACK and Littlejack and Stragg and Strugg and all their men scattered through the castle like a band of mad baboons, and their shouting and their clamour shook the shields upon the walls. 'Find the jewels or the map!' cried Black and Littlejack. 'Find the jewels or the map!' shouted Stragg and Strugg and all their men. And they used their axes and their cudgels on every lock and every door, breaking into cupboards, cracking open closets, prying off the lids of boxes, smashing clocks with spades. The hours went on and the clangour rose. Everything that had an O was opened, ransacked, and pulled apart – sofas, and couches, and otto-mans, things made of onyx and ormolu, ivory and ebony, gold and chalcedony, crocks and bowls, pillows and cushions and footstools, and even flagons and goblets. The men drank wine from bottles, white and red and *rosé*, and then they smashed the bottles. Boards were taken up, and marble floors, but no jewels came to light, or any map, no glow or gleam or glitter, no sight of parchment.

The moon went down; the sun began to climb the heavens. The clamour and the clangour ceased. Everything that could be broken had been broken. Glass and splinters, bits and fragments lay upon the floors, or where the floors had been. Then the wild-eyed Black raised his clenched gloves to-wards the sky and in that moment saw the map. It hung upon a wall, the only one left standing.

'I have not seen this wall before,' cried Black.

'It was not here a moment since,' cried Littlejack. 'I'd lay to that.'

They took the map down from the wall and spread it on a plank and bent above it, and in the end deciphered all its marks and crosses.

'The treasure lies five thousand feet from where this skull is grinning,' shouted Black. 'We come first to a stricken oak and count off fifty paces.'

'Nor', nor'east,' cried Littlejack.

'The jewels are ours,' Black gloated. 'We're princes!'

'Kings!' bawled Littlejack. And Stragg and Strugg and all their men echoed 'Kings!' But there was no echo to their echo, for all the walls were gone. They saw before them now a dark and gloomy forest, stretching on and on, and on and farther.

'Spades!' commanded Black. 'And follow me!' Then each man seized his spade and followed Black and Littlejack and Stragg and Strugg into the dark and gloomy forest.

'How goes the day?' cried Black.

'It lacks two hours of noon,' said Littlejack.

'I hate the sound of noon,' said Black. 'I know not why.'

'Perhaps because it has two O's,' said Stragg.

'Perhaps because the day grows hot,' said Strugg.

'And treasure should be dug up in the night,' said Littlejack.

'Silence,' thundered Black, 'and follow me. The weather here is strange. I hate this weather.'

'Why is it so hard', asked Littlejack, 'to stay together?' And even as he spoke he found himself alone. He called and got no answer.

'This way,' cried Black, 'and all men follow me. I feel the jewels burning in my hands. I have the map and a compass. Find the stricken oak!' His voice ended in a gurgle and a croak. And then his eyes grew wide with fear, his fingers trembled, for he stood all alone, like all the others. The going underfoot was slow and oozy, for burrowing moles had devoured the roots and softened the soil.

'There are no outlets and no openings,' cried Black. 'It's soggy and it's boggy.'

A million moths hovered above his shoulders and countless chameleons changed colour on gloomy growths. Glow-worms glowed around and about, and Black could not make out where he was going. Then came the butterflies. 'Butterflies do not have O's,' cried Black, but he was wrong. The monarchs and the morning cloaks, the clouded yellows, and all their colleagues and their fellows made up the throng. The sun went out and it seemed night again.

'What is this woeful wood?' Black whimpered, and no one answered.

'What is this woeful wood?' croaked Littlejack, lost and all alone in another part of the forest. The dark was deep as midnight all around. 'Whence comes this humming and this buzzing?' wailed Littlejack. And then he saw the source of the ominous sounds: locusts and hornets and dragonflies, yellow-jackets and honey-bees. They came in clouds and hosts and squadrons. 'Black never thought of *little* things', mourned Littlejack, 'when he was issuing edicts.' He groped his way slowly into an outlandish grove, but there his way was clogged by a growth of toadstools and mushrooms and monkshood and bloodroot, foxglove, wolf-bane and aconite, orchids and opium poppies, and the roots of mandragora. Spanish moss drooped down and Spanish bayonets shot up. 'What are these woeful worts?' muttered Littlejack, now up to his ankles and his knees in worts: bloodwort, dragonwort, goutwort, hogwort, holewort, hoodwort, lousewort, moonwort, moorwort, scorpionwort, throatwort, toothwort, and woundwort.

'What woeful wood is this?' squealed Hyde, lost and all alone in another part of the forest. Odd lights blinded him with their glow and glare and glitter: St Elmo's fire and foxfire, will-o'-the-wisp and phosphorus, and the aurora borealis. 'These are the lights of night, and not of day,' moaned Hyde, 'and yet I thought I saw the dawn a few hours since.' He stared up at the sky, seeking the sun, and the cold O of Canopus stared down at him. The Southern Cross seemed to point its stars at him like fingers, comets and meteors flared like flaming arrows, and Virgo blazed, Capricorn, and Scorpio, the Major Dogstar and the Minor, and so many others, Hyde lost count of stars and constellations.

Then the lights went out and darkness reigned once more, and in the darkness came a show of fireworks: rockets dropping colourful balloons,

Roman candles, flowerpots, and golden showers, and silver fountains. And now there were owls and crows, loons and woodcocks, herons and flamingoes, cormorants and condors, and one albatross with an arrow from a crossbow in its feathers, swooping and stooping about his head like bombers. He stumbled on, plagued by a scourge of mosquitoes, microbes, and micro-organisms, through sycamore and hemlock, cottonwood and hickory, black and honey locust, oak and giant redwood, and underfoot, frogs and toads in woad hindered and hampered and harassed his going. 'Incompetent, irrelevant, and immaterial,' he murmured, and all the other lawyer talk that lawyers talk in triplicate. Suddenly a swoop of swans attacked him. 'Objection!' Hyde implored. 'Swans have no O's.' Then he recalled the cob and cos, or male and female swan. 'Confusion on creatures without an O that have an O in their alias,' shouted Hyde, and even as he spoke a lynx was snarling at his feet. 'The bobcat,' whimpered Hyde. A puma showed its gleaming fangs. 'The mountain lion,' quavered Hyde. 'But here's a camel! I can ride!'

'I am the dromedary,' the camel said, or seemed

to say, and then it closed one eye, and opened it, and went away.

'Imponderable, impalpable, and improbable,' shouted Hyde. A nightingale beat its wings before his eyes. '*Je suis le rossignol*,' it sang.

'Impossible,' raved Hyde, 'irreverent, and unfair.'

Three bears transpired, in legal lingo, which means they happened, took place, and occurred. '*Les ours*, in French!' Hyde screamed. 'Moreover, furthermore, and too: the cinnamon, the polar, and the brown.' He took four wobbly hops and toppled and fell down.

8

ALL of a sudden the way grew clearer for Black in his dark part of the forest, and the sun shone bright. The earth beneath his feet seemed firmer. The threatening trees had disappeared except for one, all that was left of a stricken oak, standing in a clearing. And then he saw the long gaunt form of Littlejack, and Stragg and Strugg, and all their men, gathered about a certain spot and pointing with their spades, bitten and stung, and ruffled and rumpled, but screaming in glee and delight.

'This is the place!' cried Littlejack.

'Dig,' croaked Black. And the men were about to dig with their spades, but their hands were stayed as they raised them by an ominous clamour and clangour, a snow of arrows and a sound of armour. Many figures of men loomed up, afoot or on horses, and they rode and ran among the crew, and the crew let drop their spades.

'These are but figures of fantasy,' cried Black. 'These men have no blood in their veins.'

'Dig,' bawled Littlejack, but no man dug. They stood as if rooted in the ground and gazed at the apparitions.

'Ink runs in their veins, immortal ink, the ink of song and story.' It was the voice of Andreus.

'Ink can be destroyed,' cried Black, 'and men who are made of ink. Name me their names!'

They came so swiftly from the skies Andreus couldn't name them all, streaming out of lore and legend, streaming out of song and story, each phantom flaunting like a flag his own especial glory: Lancelot and Ivanhoe, Athos, Porthos, Cyrano, Roland, Rob Roy, Romeo; Donalbane of Birnam Wood, Robinson Crusoe and Robin Hood; the moody Doones of *Lorna Doone*, Davy Crockett and Daniel Boone; out of near and ancient tomes, Banquo's ghost and Sherlock Holmes; Lochinvar, Lothario, Horatius, and Horatio; and there were other figures, too, darker, coming from the blue, Shakespeare's Shylock, Billy Bones, Quasimodo, Conrad's Jones, Ichabod and Captain Hook – names enough to fill a book.

'These wearers of the O, methinks, are indestructible,' wailed Littlejack.

'Books can be burned,' croaked Black.

'They have a way of rising out of ashes,' said Andreus.

'I have a woeful feeling, as if the double O of doom were sticking in my throat.' Black's voice, though choked, grew brighter. 'The phantoms pass,' he cried. 'Take up your spades!' But as if this were a signal or sign, the air was filled with sudden laughter, and other figures began circling above and about the vandals like laughing Indians riding ponies, led by Mother Goose astride a broom.

'Who are these spawn of nightmare or of fever?' demanded Black.

This time it was Andrea's voice that answered him: 'Little Jack Horner come out of his corner, Tommy Trout and the cat he pulled out, poor Cock Robin and Bessy Brooks, Simple Simon and Tommy Snooks, Dr Foster come home from Gloucester, Little Boy Blue and King Cole, too, and a certain old woman who lived in a shoe.'

'These are but shadows,' quavered Black. 'I ripped the O from heroes and from fools!'

'But not from love,' said Andrea, 'or from affection, and not from memory or recollection.'

'Pick up your spades!' ordered Black, laughing so his men would laugh, but no one laughed. Then other shadows rode like thunder from the skies: the Argonauts and Myrmidons and Amazons, Adonis and Endymion, Apollo and Hyperion, and high above them, flying faster, Pollux and his brother Castor, burning like a flame in spars, lighting up the sky like stars.

Then came the great O giants: Cormoran and Blunderbore, Goliath and a hundred more, the

Cyclops, hurling peaks at Noman, and even the Abominable Himalayan Snowman.

The men were prostrate now upon the ground, and all their eyes were closed against the visions from the sky.

'Dig,' croaked Black, 'or I shall slay you!' He drew his pistol from his belt, and Littlejack his cutlass. Fearing death far more than apparition, the men began to dig, and as they dug, a clock began to strike, an unseen clock. The earth was suddenly hard and cold, and the blades of spades were bent and broken. 'You've struck a chest,' cried Black, 'an ironbound chest and oaken.' But what the men had struck was carbonate and carborundum, conglomerate or puddingstone and something known as oolite or dogger. The clock continued striking. 'I destroyed all clocks,' cried Black.

'All clocks save one,' said Andreus, 'the clock that strikes in conscience.' The deep tones of the clock went on until the clock had struck eleven. And on this stroke a curious phenomenon occurred. Upon the ground, and all around, appeared a score of objects, each one different from the others.

'Containers!' Black's voice was hollow. 'I should have destroyed containers, and the things contained therein. A curse on Hyde and his collective nouns!'

'What is in these things I do not know, but not a single one of them contains an O.' Littlejack's voice was bleak as he gazed at the odd collection: a chest, a trunk, a valise, and all sorts of cases, a barrel, a bag, and a bin, and all sorts of vases.

'A sack, a bucket, and a basket,' cried Black, 'a crate, an urn, and even a casket.' His eyes grew dark and then they lit with a fiendish lightning. 'The jewels!' he cried. 'The precious stones!'

And Black and Littlejack, and Stragg and Strugg and all their men began opening the O-less containers, and in each one they found a single sheet of paper. And on each sheet a single word appeared, that gleamed and glowed and glittered. The clock struck twelve.

'It's noon,' cried Black, and all the people echoed, 'Noon!'

Then they heard the ringing of a distant bell, sounding near and sounding nearer, ringing clear and ringing clearer, till all the sky was filled with music as by magic.

'Freedom!' Andreus cried, naming the gleaming word the men had found, the word that glowed and glittered.

'Freedom!' Andrea echoed after him, and the sound of the greatest word turned the vandals pale and made them tremble.

'I knew the word could not be doom,' the old man said, 'or sorrow. I was afraid that it might be tomorrow.'

9

AND then, as by a miracle of motion, the
vandals stood upon the shore, and all the
people of the island stood about them.
'Your hour has struck,' said Andreus. 'Here is
your ship. Begone.'

'The gangway and the decks are oozy with

oysters!' cried Black, 'and Portuguese men-of-war, and lobsters, and an octopus. And swordfish are sawing something below the waterline, urged on by a horrid school of chortling porpoises!'

Hyde was suddenly up to his ankles in phantas-magoria. 'Crabs, crayfish, prawns, shrimps,' he howled, 'alias the decapods. Centipedes and spiders, alias the arthropods. Snails and slugs, alias molluscs and gastropods.' He thought he saw crickets, too, alias orthoptera, and a score of zooming bats, alias chiroptera. He turned and ran, pursued by rodents small and big, the rat, the rabbit, and the guinea-pig.

The unseen clock struck one. 'The mouse is running down the clock. I see him run,' said Littlejack. And all the crew saw things that weren't there as they clambered aboard the ship and set her gloomy sails, and headed slowly out to sea. And then, beyond the far horizon, the great O storms began to rage and roar, the hurricanes,* the typhoon and the monsoon, the cyclone and tornado, and there were cloudbursts and water-spouts and fog and snow, and whirlpools and maelstroms, and other odd phenomena, each

*Connie, Dorothy and Flora, Imogene and Josephine and Nora.

with its O. The night came on and in the light of lightning there were those on shore who saw, or thought they saw, the head of the giant Orion rising out of the sea. And there were those on shore who saw, or thought they saw, the vengeful ships of the great explorers: Columbus, De Soto, Cortez, and Balboa, and all of the others since Jason and since Noah.

No word was ever heard of Black or Littlejack again, or Stragg or Strugg, or any of their men. A broken spar was washed upon the shore one day, and one black glove, but that was all. The outlawed lawyer Hyde, looking for a loophole in the law through which he might escape, was caught in one whose O's collapsed and buried him beneath its wreckage. And as he fell he heard another O, sounded by an old owl in a mossy oak, a little like an oboe obbligato.

10

WORKING with valour and love and hope,
the islanders put the O back in everything
that had lost it. The name of Goldilocks
regained its laughter, and there were locks for
keys, and shoes were no longer shes. A certain
couple once more played their fond duets on man-

dolin and glockenspiel. Ophelia Oliver, who had
vanished from the haunts of men, returned, wearing
both her O's again. Otto Ott could say his
name without a stammer, and dignity returned
to human speech and English grammar. Once
more a man could say boo to a goose, and tell the
difference between to lose and too loose. Every
family had again a roof and floor, and the head of
the house could say in English, as before: 'Someone open (or close) the door.' Towers rose up
again and fountains sparkled. In the spring the
robin and the oriole returned. The crows were
loud in caucus, and the whippoorwill sang once
again at night. The wounds that Black and Littlejack had made were healed by morning-glories,
columbine, and clover, and a spreading comforter
of crocuses. One April morning, Andreus and
Andrea were wed.

'It could have been worse,' the old man said,
riding back home from the wedding. 'They might
have taken A. Then we would have had no marriage, or even carriage, or any walks to walk on.'
He wiped a tear from his eye. He was worrying
about the loss of I, if I had been forbidden, when
he came upon the lovers in a garden. 'What

would have happened,' he asked them both, 'without indivisibility?'

'Or, for the matter of that,' said Andreus, 'invincible?'

'Invincible', the old man said, 'is a matter of O.'

'What O?' asked Andreus and Andrea together.

'The O, lest we forget,' the old man said, 'in freedom.'

Suddenly their thoughtful silence was changed to laughter. 'Squck his thrug,' they heard the parrot squawking.

'He must have missed the ship,' said Andrea.

'And now he has the freedom of screech,' said Andreus.

And they took the green parrot into their cottage, and in the end he was squawking, 'Watch the sea!' And whenever they heard this warning and alarm, the islanders sprang to their ramparts and their towers, and scanned the sea for sinister ships with sinister sails.

Many years went by, and then one day a very old man with a long white beard stood at the base of a towering shaft of marble, surmounted, high up in the sky, with a single letter of the alphabet that glowed and gleamed and glittered in every light and weather.

'What a strange statue,' a little boy cried. 'A statue to a circle.'

'What a strange monument,' a little girl laughed. 'A monument to zero.'

The old man sighed and scratched his head, and thought and thought, and then he said, 'It has a curious and wondrous history.'

'Was it a battle? And did we win?' the children cried.

The old man shook his head and sighed, 'I'm not as young as I used to be, and the years gone by are a mystery, but 'twas a famous victory.'

The sun went down, and its golden glow lighted with fire the wonderful O.

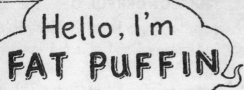

Hello, I'm **FAT PUFFIN**

Would YOU like to find out more about Puffin books and authors, enter competitions and get a chance to buy new books?

Then join The Puffin Club!

You will get a copy of the Club magazine four times a year, a membership book and a badge.

And there's lots more! For further details and an application form send a stamped, addressed envelope to:

The Puffin Club Dept. A
Penguin Books Ltd.,
Bath Road,
Harmondsworth,
Middlesex UB7 0DA

If you live in AUSTRALIA write to: The Australian Puffin Club, Penguin Books Australia Ltd., P.O. Box 257, Ringwood, Victoria 3134